THE TENDERNESS OF STONE

A Memoir

Ira Heinrich

VOLUME ONE
of
LORD OF THE VALLEY

Giri Marga Press
Portland, Oregon

Copyright © 2007 by Ira Heinrich. All Rights Reserved
ISBN 978-0-6151-8695-5

Cover image Copyright © 2007 by Brian Hausback, California State University, Sacramento, used with permission.

Acknowledgements

I wish to offer thanks to the following people for their contributions to this book: My old friend and colleague Walt Anderson helped me taxonomically and with skillful, indispensable editing, but his very early words of encouragement and confidence in the story were a contribution of much greater importance. Leslie Pfardresher kindly offered up her editing and consultation time and her initial response to the material may have helped save it from oblivion. Aaron Heinrich gave his willing spirit and hours of his time in taking the manuscript and helping me make it into a book. My brother in spirit Jose' Freeman, in sharing the Giri-Marga with me, has for many years made subtle and profound contributions to this writing. The late Professor Mirceau Eliade twenty years ago gave me some words of advice that greatly informed the book's direction.

And I must recognize those who see themselves in the background of this story and although unnamed, will probably know who they are.

-I.H.

For Bonnie Bee

I

It is as if my birth, my emergence from womb to world, had taken place somehow just here, at the foot of this small island of eroded volcanic crags piercing the level soil in the very center of the great valley.

It is as if they shed some persistently penetrative light, not to be deflected or resisted, that pierced the womb wherein I had been planted, a light like tentacles, like soft grasping hands that struck me there within, before my life had begun, hands of light that caught me, clutched me, pulled me out, suddenly, shockingly into the world.

It is as if the very first vision presented to my new eyes was this small mountain, as if seeing it blaze up before me as my new life's first and primary image, all of my years were shaped in that instant of birth-sight, rendered in the image of that mountain, that level earth pulled, twisted and sprung upward from the center of the plain, setting apart high from low, form from space, wildness from cultivation, dream from sleep, love from loss, life from death, and in separating heaven from earth like this, created and revealed the whole world.

***

    I believe I dreamed during most of that long drive with my father through the California night when, as profoundly and as innocently unknowing as an infant being born, I passed from simple childhood into the light and shadow of awaiting myth.

    In my father's enthusiasm for our northern California destination, he was effusive in his description of our new life to come and the new land that excited and inspired him. He talked ceaselessly to me, not noticing that I was half-asleep, while he drove north through the San Joaquin toward the Sacramento Valley. His factual narrative produced a procession of fantastic images in my restless dreams: I saw huge sweet-smelling peaches hanging from mammoth trees stretching in endless rows beneath turquoise skies; crystalline water gushing from artesian springs and flooding boundless orchards; and I was running through vast fields of berries and grain, sailing through darkling clouds above it all surrounded by a phalanx of migrating swans.

    Then there was a tall, white, moonlit house nested in a jungle of gnarled trees, its many, many antique windows shinning like rippled mirrors in the night. In my dream I saw this old mansion from the sky among the piping swans, and I descended with breathtaking swiftness to a lawn before a massive porch where a mockingbird sang a strange melody on an ornate light post out front. And then oddly, there was the grinding of gravel and the slamming of a car door. I awoke suddenly, and with sleepy eyes saw that the house was not a dream, and we had arrived late in the full-moon night at our dark, empty new home. While I blinked in my lingering drowsiness, my hyperactive father was already pulling the mattresses from the trailer. "Hey, lazybones! Wake up, we're home!" Blindly, in the night, as yet an unknowing child, I had arrived in the shadow of a mystery.

Two years before, I had drifted to sleep on the highway somewhere between Nebraska and California, piled into the station-wagon with my siblings and parents, pelting across the country to some sort of new life in the West, my irrepressible father at the wheel singing his favorite traveling song: *"You are my sunshine, my only sunshine, you make me happy when skies are gray, you'll never know dear how much I love you, please don't take my sunshine away,"* and enthusing over the California to come. We were headed for Los Angeles, but we were country people, and the fascinating nightmare of that grotesque, sprawling city was never more than a necessary interlude. My father took his young family there reluctantly while he prepared to practice his profession in a proper environment and searched in the fruited garden of California for just the right place to build a new life and raise his family. But we had to first spend two difficult years in an alien, urban environment that was deeply distasteful to my Midwestern parents, an environment that was a necessary nightmare to my countried, cornfield family.

Los Angeles was a brief tangle of a life for me. I bicycled through strange Pasadena neighborhoods, walked to school in the morning not understanding why I could not take a full breath without coughing, explored old suburban neighborhoods and parks and gardens, like Griffith Park, Santa Anita, Huntington Gardens, and the bizarre La Brea Tar Pits. This urban landscape, sprinkled with exotic palm trees, smelled strangely of odd plants and shrubbery, so unlike the Nebraska cornfields where I had grown to boyhood.

We were not to stay there long. Los Angeles was only a vacuous interruption of several generations of prairie farm life. My parents would inevitably return to the familiar tradition of their rural history. In a box-like house with peeling paint rising from a Kansas knoll, my mother had been born amid my grandmother's chicken-house and milking cows. In rolling fields nearby my grandfather putted through his corn on the old John Deere. Mom played with rocks and puppies in the dusty yard while she grew. She is over eighty now but I still treasure an old rocking chair on which her little feet wore still-seen indentations as she rocked herself by the stove, listening to tornado reports and gospel music on the Wichita radio station.

Six hundred miles to the north, my father spent much of his boyhood under the watchful eye of his weather-beaten dad, rolling endless rocks off wheat fields that were being carved from the North Dakota prairie. A quarter section away from the struggling wheat field in the virgin prairie stood a squat one-story house and a snow-whipped barn. In the frigid North Dakota wind they clung to the sod near a glacial lake where my grandmother broke the ice in the cistern and carried water to the house.

And at a Christian college of tall red-bricked buildings in a Nebraska village halfway between Stutsman County North Dakota, and Marion County Kansas, my parents had met, married and started a family. At five or six, I began to amble over the brick streets from the soda shop to the butcher shop where I amused the butchers John and Mike with accounts of fantastic adventures. At seven, my barefoot pals and I found a dirty hog shed standing in the middle of a muddy pond, to us like a castle in a moat. Every day we walked through a mile of broken corn, rested underneath the only tree in the section, then slopped through the mud to the hog shed and performed now-forgotten boyhood rituals of play.

We were country people and not long for Los Angeles. But my father had a vision of another kind of farmland than the rolling, tattered expanses of the Great Plains. As a child he had tiptoed into the kitchen on Christmas morning breathlessly anticipating something exotic, sublime and rare in his knitted stocking. It was an orange. Now, after two alien years in Los Angeles, he was leaving behind the land where oranges were miracles and taking his young family to the center of a five-thousand square mile garden as flat as a table top where oranges and every other kind of fruit you could imagine grew in orchards stretching as far as the eye could see.

And that evening as we rolled down off the Grape Vine onto the old narrow two-lane highway 99, I had gotten glimpses of the cotton fields and hot-dog stands of the San Joaquin Valley until nightfall blacked out the endless agriculture and shabby towns and left us scooting in a flat, straight line through the dark. Except for the lights of gas stations and intersections, that long drive through the night was devoid of impressions except one: *flatness*, unremitting and hypnotizing flatness. I drifted into dream with an image of a land with absolutely no boundaries where the unvarying level merged with a hazy horizon a thousand miles away.

Sometime during the night, I awoke to the lurching of the car and the sudden silencing of the motor. "Here we are," my dad said huskily. Through the car window I could see the dim form of the large, tall house glowing faintly white amidst twisted trees. Even in his exhaustion, my dad's agitated energy rose to the surface, and while I struggled to rub the sleep from my eyes, he had bounded from the car.

I don't believe I ever really woke up as I stumbled out of the car, and stood wavering on the gravel driveway before the old country house my father had acquired for us on a previous trip here alone. In the dim beam of the headlights, I saw the rough outline of an old barn not far down the driveway behind the house. We walked together in the moonlight down the drive. My dad wanted me to see the barn. I could smell musty hay thickly in the warm air. A massive oak leaned over the barn's roof, and something white and winged rose from a branch and with a shriek like a frightened child, passed over our heads making clicking sounds as it flew.

The key worked only in the front door, so we stumbled around to the front of the house. There was a vague sense of a densely treed expanse beyond us. The screen door squeaked loudly. Dad bumped into something in the dark, flashed his light on it and I saw an old porch swing stir to a wobbling orbit on rusty chains. His key was in the door and it swung open before us. A breath of cool air passed my face. It was old air, heavy with the age of the room. The ceiling was too high to see in the blackness. A wooden floor squeaked under our feet. "Wait here," said my dad. "I'll get the mattresses," and I was alone for a minute or two in the empty room. On my left I could see a large fireplace, mantle higher than my head. On my right dimly through a high door, a staircase rose into the black above. On glass panes above the doors an old pioneer grandmother had hand-painted scenes of a pastoral grace now long gone. The house was full of squeaks and groans.

Five minutes later I was crawling into a sleeping bag next to my dad. After the exhausting drive, he fell asleep almost at once but I turned on my back and lay staring upward. I could not see the ceiling, but near the center of the room, a very large and elaborate chandelier, installed by the prosperous California fruit-growing pioneers who had built the old house in 1872, hung suspended in the dense black, its crystals just touched by a dim light that slanted through high windows from somewhere outside. Perhaps our entering and stirring had produced a bit of breeze, for the chandelier began to swing, pendulum-like, rhythmic and eerie, back and forth, squeaking faintly with each pass. Later, intrigued by this first-night image, I wrote a juvenile novel entitled *The Mystery of the Swinging Chandelier*. But now, still in the foggy dream of half-sleep, I barely knew where I was. I watched the chandelier with a thick, slow sort of fascination. Each swing erased a bit of my waking consciousness but there remained some undefined sense of deep apprehension.

I felt disturbed by the dark night, by the old dark house filled with strange sounds and musty smells. Somehow I already missed my short, uncomplicated life, unfolded in the thoughtlessness of a cornfield boyhood. Gentle, simply religious, countrified parents had poured over me the milk of a love without boundaries or conditions. I had known the world only as the organic reality of my extended German agrarian family, as firm as the Nebraska prairie where I had been born

In the morning, that neat little level life was to be pierced and changed forever, and although innocent of what was to come, I felt a vague sense of uneasiness hovering about me in the blackness. But now I was rocked as in an old cradle in that old house beneath that antique chandelier into a deep, dreamless and unexpecting sleep.

There were owls living in a hole in the oak that hovered over the barn and in the dim light of early dawn they wheeled silently from their nest over the tall house, calling a farewell to the night. I awoke to their raspy screeching and lay still a moment, wondering first what had made the sound, then wondering where I was. As sometimes happens in the fresh and untainted lives of children, the progression of time and its sequence of events collapsed in this moment of waking. Lost to me was the fact of my family's journey from the plains of the Midwest to the foreignness of California. Gone was that brief geographical particularity, that bizarre *exoticus* of Los Angeles. As I awoke that morning, there remained only the most tenuous sense of a life previous to this strange re-birth. I knew I was somehow beginning again, and I found myself greeting with excitement and not a little fear, an unknown world that was waiting for me. The vaulted room was in shadow. My father breathed heavily beside me. The chandelier was still. There was a sweet pungency to the air that I would learn to recognize later as the bouquet of ripening peaches in the morning mist of summer. A narrow band of amber sunlight now reached over the high shrub outside the window and I could see the gossamer of cobwebs glowing in the high corners. I remembered the old barn out in the dreamy night, the impression of which remained as only a fascinating suggestion.

I was not reflecting about the past, about any change in life. I was completely lost in a fascinating immediacy. In a moment, I had rolled out of the sleeping bag and was creeping through the house. I passed through a wainscoted empty dining room, passed a kitchen where a many-paned window flooded the walls with morning light, and opened a creaky door to the back porch. Screen was all that separated two walls of the room from outside, and a flood of new smells enveloped me, smells of fruit, irrigation water stewing on rich black soil, pine, oak, pomegranate and flowered shrubs, all seen mottled through the screen. One wall was lined with shelves as high as the ceiling. I noticed the rings of canning jars imprinted in the ancient paint.

At the back screen door, I could see a cement walk leading through what seemed almost a tunnel of foliage. Dimly, on the right, a tall, square building rose at the end of the walk three stories into the trees, its sides of mottled wood-shakes a weathered gray. The light of morning now touched its upper reaches with a soft red blush.

Although nearly the whole night drive had been a dream to me, there remained, like the narrative of that dream, my father's vivid descriptions of the huge garden of the Sacramento Valley, the miles of peaches, walnuts, almonds, prunes and grain, perfectly manicured fields neatly divided into tidy squares, where cultivation was unimpeded by prairie rocks or irregularity of any kind. As he had talked, I had gazed into the black night through half-closed eyes, seeing in my sleepy musing the dark edges of the fields he was describing, feeling vividly the utter flatness of the land under our rolling car. I had an image of a place somewhat like the rowed vegetable gardens I was used to, except of gigantic proportions, stretching on and on, with row-crops as big as trees extending like a maze outward in all directions.

Now all of this, all of this dreaming, all of this undefined transformation that I felt happening in my limited little life, was coming to a concentrated focus in the walk that led between these two lines of high bushes rank and long unpruned, so fully had my short history disappeared, so completely was my attention limited to the moment at hand. In the early morning, the pavement was in deep shadow as the foliage leaned overhead to nearly obscure the sky. The walk and its tunnel of shadow were the perfect metaphor for the narrowed aperture of my life on that particular morning, and as if to complete the image, there was, at the end of the dark stretch of pavement, a round patch of dazzling light so bright it hurt my eyes, glowing where the path opened onto the small field between the yard and the barn. I was keeping my eyes cast down from the glare, except when I glanced up at the square, tower-like building that stood three stories high at the right end of the walk. Reaching the last of the pavement, I squinted and looked up for my first view of the great level garden of the valley that was to be my home, half dream, half memory of my father's descriptions.

My dad had never even mentioned "mountains" as part of his passionate profile of the immense, fertile valley he had chosen for our new life. During our two years in L.A., he had scanned every nook and cranny of the California wonderland, searching for just the right place for us. He had considered places like San Luis Obispo, Santa Inez, Santa Barbara, the whole expanse of the San Joaquin, Sacramento, Santa Rosa, Tehama and Shasta counties, even the Willamette Valley of Oregon. But in considering these areas, he always looked only at *valleys*. Cultivation, tillability, agricultural fertility—all of his life these were the qualities that gave real value to any landscape. Mountains were merely scenic boundaries, the inevitable margins of *real* land to him. Of all the profusely varied landscapes of California he had chosen Sutter County, in an act strangely fated for me, as the absolute ideal, the only county in California that does not extend to the Great Valley's mountainous margin. Therefore there was no reason whatsoever why my expectation of our new homeland, created by my father's vivid descriptions, should include mountains of any kind.

So in that first gaze, squinting into the uncomfortable light of that dazzling summer morning just at the edge of our jungled yard, I was absolutely shocked to see an utterly unearthly cluster of jagged peaks abruptly rising completely out of place, over the level orchards only a few miles away.

Even today, so many years later, it is difficult for me to grasp fully what happened to my consciousness at this concussion. There are many ancient stories from the sacred lands of India of unsuspecting neophytes whose minds are vacated and neutralized by the sudden appearance of their particular spiritual master. There are other stories about overzealous sadhu-masters recognizing likely child-disciples and throwing hypnotizing powder into their eyes, befuddling them and carrying them off for further initiation. My experience when I saw this crowd of peaks for the first time was something like this. For a brief but overpowering moment, I forgot utterly who was this small boy that I had known myself to be. Before this I had lived the conventional, unconsidered life of a child, but suddenly all of that child's little imaginings, enthusiasms and agonies were gone. This is most difficult of explanation, but in that moment my sense of deepest identity merged with and became identical with the Being of that solitary mountain. For just an instant, I was more familiar with myself than I had ever been, but it was not the *self* I had always known. That small boy had without warning emerged from a mild and gentle childhood into the morning of an utterly new and unpredictable life, a life to be wrenched off the wide and level path laid out by fundamentalist culture and circumstances of birth.

Then, just as suddenly, this familiar but frightening sensation evaporated like the mist that hung over the peach orchards all around, and I felt the sense of my own body again and within it felt my child's mind struggling to begin considering not only what had just happened to me, but struggling to see and grasp that isolated cluster of pinnacles that had so violently transfixed my attention.

In a fever of anticipation to get a better view, I thought at once of the old tower rising to my right. An extension of the walkway skirted the rear of the building where it led to a rickety stairway shambling up to a door, tilting crazily off its hinges at the second story. On the way to the stair, I passed a strange, squat little shed with a small half-sized door. I peered inside and was overcome with the scent of musty earth. I realized this was the shaft of an old well and had some vague idea that the well and the adjacent tower were related. Indeed, the well had once supplied water to an elevated tank in the tower. In the days to come, I was often to climb down into that well, digging and burrowing tunnels and caves into the fragrant earth as boys are wont to do, oblivious of the danger involved. There I would nestle in the dark warmth of little nest-like rooms I had secretly excavated. But now there burned vividly in my mind an image of a tower of rock, a landscape like the moon, a landscape that had shocked me into a state of single-mindedness. I scrambled up the stairs and crept into the room of the second floor.

The walls had once been whitewashed but were stained now with pigeon droppings and great age. Amazingly, the floor was strewn with papers and books from several decomposed boxes that had burst open. I poked about in the papers and was able to perceive that they were receipts, business records, letters. Dusty and blackened faces peered from a few very old photographs through the thick patina of grime and corrosion that had accumulated on them. I knew I would take a closer look at them later. One of the old books was a diary. I pried it away from the dust and mold, leaving pieces of the cover on the floor, and sat cross-legged in the dust while I curiously turned over a few pages and tried to make out the faded writing. The entry I noticed was dated December of 1890, and in his antiquated cursive a pioneer father was recounting a harrowing buggy-ride through the rising water of the Butte Sink, wending his way through tules higher than his mules' heads, struggling to make it home to his family, waiting there before the fireplace, in this old house, for Christmas eve. Dimly aware of how remarkable it was that this old family memorabilia had been abandoned there, I knew I would look into that later, as well.

Now my attention was attracted by a vertical ladder nailed to the studs of the walls. Up I climbed, disturbing a coating of dust that must have remained intact for a generation or more. At the top of the ladder, I had to crawl, balanced on my hands and knees, over a narrow plank placed across the rafters. Fat pigeons murmured in the corners and rustled into motion, reluctant to move. At the center of the building, where two of these planks crossed, about three feet above me, a sort of narrow hatch let out onto the peaked roof of the tower. I could see the square patch of blue summer sky through the hole.

As I had turned this way and that, searching for the best grip for hands and feet, I had momentarily lost my sense of direction so that when I hoisted myself onto the high roof I was slightly dizzy with no clear idea which way to look for those unearthly mountains I had so briefly seen a few minutes before. My head swam a little as I scanned an expanse that seemed unbelievably wide. The surface of the world below was made up of an uninterrupted grid, criss-crossed, cross-hatched, checkerboard squares of an infinite variety of sizes, the intersections composed of all manner of linear patterns. These were the rows, thousands of rows, of the great garden of the Sacramento Valley, varied by half-a-dozen different kinds of orchard trees, as many types of row crops, as well as closely spaced troughs created by a thousand tractors tracing their lines in soils of a varying amber tone and texture. Here and there at the corners and occasionally right in the middle of some distant field, there stood a patch of yard trees surrounding a house, each with a barn or two nearby, tin roofs gleaming like mirrors in the morning sun. Most were presided over by a contorted oak, like the barn and tree of our own acreage just below. I was baffled by the absolute linearity of it all. In the Nebraska farm country where I had been born the cornfield rows were gently and everywhere curved by the rolling contour of the land. But here there seemed to be no relief from straightness. The world was an endless pattern of unbending lines, many hued by the produce, grain and fruit that grew there, but unbending nevertheless. A kind of monotony of perception fell over me, the more oppressive after the startling visual catharsis I had experienced below with my sudden discovery of those unexpected mountains.

I took all this in during the space of a moment as I scanned the horizon. I had been gazing toward the south, and my eyes swept to the right, westward. Almost immediately I felt a profound, imposing *presence*. My gaze fell fully upon the serrated line of that cluster of jagged peaks, crowded together, their heads, some pointed, some rounded, leaning crazily toward each other. They rose almost explosively right out of an otherwise uninterrupted plain of orchard and grain. I could see the expanse of the valley sweeping around them both to the south and the north. I could see that they stood absolutely alone, as if they had been dropped from space, a strange cosmic piece of geography interrupting the regularity, the organization, the careful cultivation of the vast valley of the Sacramento. They stood there in the midst of all that order, wild and fierce, an overpowering mass of irregularity and curve, a huge untamed patch of compelling shadow and sun-gleaming texture. There were many peaks towering together like a tall family, and I noticed as I took that first long look the subtle variation in the shade of each peak, suggesting the spaces between. The dark clefts pulled on me with terrific force. My thoughts swam with vague barely formed images of misty canyons and fantastic shapes. I thought I could see gleams and sparkles in the huge massifs of their summits. I felt a surging feeling in my midsection. I was being swept into the sky by the mountains' rising. I felt as if they had just now pierced the earth with a grand violence as I had turned my eyes there. There was a rumble and a humming in my ears.

I lay on the warm crumbling shakes of that tower's roof for a long time, my heart racing within me. My spirit wandered in stunned wonder over the mountains' complexity of golden grasslands, dotted oak woodlands and slopes of crowded chaparral. I thought I could see the shapes of individual boulders, shinning in the clear air. I was transfixed by these images until the rest of the world had disappeared, and the varied cluster of shinning peaks became constellated into one overwhelming luminosity.

I had no thoughts about all of this then. This was only a small circular cluster of volcanic peaks called "The Buttes" by thousands of people for whom they formed a most casual background to daily routines. I believe I was, so far as I can know, quite alone in such a life-changing perception of a feature thought commonplace by most of the general population. It would be many years before I would understand what had happened to me on that first morning, before I would realize how very pervasive, extreme and strange were this first encounter and the life-long experience here that was to follow.

Clinging there to the top of that old water tower, I felt a kind of love for which my little life had offered no precedent. This circular volcanic landscape fairly buffeted me with the power of its personality. I felt its arms reaching for me, felt myself drawn to it in a tight embrace, felt my individuality melt into its own. My whole heart flew out to it; a great and lovely Being that even then I sensed wore that rocky ragged form only as a cloak concealing a great mystery. What the costume manifested, I would gradually learn as my life there unfolded, a life that became a dance of wonder, agony and love for a place of great power whose long story was to fascinate me utterly through all the years of my life.

II

In the days of late summer that followed, the little piece of great, brooding valley occupied by our four acres of ranch house, sprawling yard, pasture and barn, took me thoroughly in and made me at home. In the second story of the rambling, century-old house, I chose a large sunroom at the western end of the upstairs, open on three walls with tall 1870's windows. An antique four-poster bed had been left in the room long ago, and it was now mine. Here I seemed to lie in the treetops, the leaves of tall Valley Oaks brushing my windows all around, whispering me to sleep. In the soft mornings I crawled through tunnels of shrubbery, sometimes sitting still and waiting until the sparrows sang around my ears. As a harbinger of what was to come, an artificial brook poured over a small mountain of volcanic rocks collected long ago from the Buttes nearby, through moss and fern to sing into the water of a wonderful fishpond, aged from its original landscaped character to a look of genuine wildness. Obese goldfish floated lazily except when they darted away to hide from hungry raccoons. I lay on the grass quietly and watched huge rats sneak from the impenetrable ivy to drink.

And then there was the tower behind the house. Although only an old decaying water tower designed and built in a different era for a practical purpose that had nothing whatsoever to do with me, I am astounded now when I reflect on what an unlikely, almost contrived feature of my new world this was. It was like a set on the stage of a play. At its base was the wide well, a cavern where I burrowed into the rich, pungent earth of the valley itself, a simple, basic, unelaborated foundation to everything that was above. In the rafters of the first floor just above, I found, in ignorance and innocence, the beautiful meditations and fancies of visionaries like Emerson, Shakespeare, Hawthorne, Dickens, Austen, Muir, Thoreau and Twain, contained in beautiful language and ornate, seductive bindings. Scattered on the floor above those rafters were the remnant documents of a Sacramento Valley pioneer family, carelessly random, disorganized, fascinating and waiting for study. And then, a few feet above all of this was a narrow portal to a high, precarious summit, a doorway to the sky where the full, sweeping grandeur of the Great Valley could be seen as the supporting context of it all, and the brooding dream of the Mountain offered a mystic disclosure of the deep meaning of everything below.

In those first months I lay across the dusty rafters and pored over the books, crept into the musty crawlspaces in the bricked and earthen basement, sneaked down the wide well behind the tower and dug tunnels in the fragrant earth. When a bewildered Ringtail fell down the chimney into the embers one evening while we were all watching Ed Sullivan and munching my dad's famous popcorn, I rescued the enchanting creature with difficulty and housed him in some old cages that stood almost hidden behind the huge pomegranate trees in the tangled yard. There he was soon joined by an injured Ross's Goose, grounded on the almost-abandoned railroad tracks that gleamed just north of the house and the old "aviary", as I called the cages. They were joined soon by a couple of cottontails, but all of these wild creatures soon made their escapes from the rickety old cages. Thirty feet away I built a strangely shaped tree house criss-crossed in the old, splitting branches of a senile walnut tree. I ventured only a few-hundred yards at a time away from the house, into green-shaded orchards. Here, branches heavy with large golden peaches, sagged almost to waist-level, and irrigation water gushed from the ground and carried a slick of leaves and dust swirling slowly around the trunks of the trees. When the moon shone, I crept to the barn and watched the owls wheeling around the top of the oak's zigzag branches, etched black against the blue glow of the sky. Living this juvenile summer life was much like poking through a vivid and fantastic picture book.

All of this had the quieting surety of home, the comforting, tightly circumscribed boundary of a child's Eden. But permeating this bucolic little home-park, a seductive and disquieting mystery lurked even in Eden, and a powerful phantom began to shimmer always before me. Like a babe attracted by a bright light over his mother's shoulder will strain against enclosing arms to see, I leaned always away from home toward the west. I was a child haunted by an ominous ghost that no one else could see.

And so every day I climbed the tower again and surrendered myself to that cluster of peaks rising in the warm air. The Place radiated tentacles of power that reached into every corner of my awareness, collected every fragment of dream, wonder and longing and pulled them all to itself. *There* was focused all that was real in me now, and it radiated that reality back with dazzling brilliance, keeping me always mindful of transcendence, keeping a great sense of mystery ever present in my thoughts.

   The Mountain invaded my dreams. I would awaken in my bed, creep down the hall past my parents' room, and climb through the attic, up a small stairway, out onto the roof of the house, bathed in a kind of sepia atmosphere, thick and buoyant. I would raise my arms, jump just a little, and slowly I would rise over the dark trees around the house, and climbing higher and higher could see through amber night the whole, grand valley stretching out, void now of orchards and barns and towns, an endless fairy-land of jungle and snaking rivers. And I would soar over the miles to those towers of rock rising from the forest at the valley's center. Strange, unspeakably lovely, twisted and wonderful were the swells and crags. Sailing high over the tallest peak, I saw huge, smooth pavilions of stone, like temple-floors, nested among the rocks at the top. (A few years later great concrete slabs were poured on that summit as floors for radio buildings, and perhaps before I die, technological obsolescence will erase the buildings, leaving only the very "pavilions" seen in my childhood dreams). Diving into the canyons to the north I skirted past towering cliffs, peering into caves that pocked the vertical walls. As I sailed by one shallow cave I saw rows of old, dusty books stacked against the rock. I soared and twisted and wheeled through the unearthly landscape of this island of volcanoes, finally turning away in weariness and returning to my bed. This dream I had many times during those first months of late summer in the valley.

   And often during those days in my room, I would interrupt my reading and go to the westward window. With my dad's binoculars in hand, I would peer and peer across the hazy distance and try to penetrate the mountainous landscape I could see compressed and foreshortened in the lens. I would be hypnotized, staring, for I sensed something or someone looking back at me, always pulling me, drawing me toward itself. (Thirty years later I would spend hours in the curvature of a small sandy cave with a southeast prospect, gazing with those same binoculars at that very window, acutely aware of the small boy gazing back at me, and the strange collapse of time involved.)

As the valley landscape about my house, variegated and unending, unfolded gradually beneath my feet, so also did the seasons and their weather unfold, but by rhythms of their own. The changes in the air were as fragrant and exotic to me as the remarkable collection of arboreal specimens in our yard. Padding in bare feet through the orchards, I watched the curling leaves of peach trees turn yellow and fall. Sitting atop the tower, I watched the summer color drain slowly from farmland below and sky above, replaced with gray. The Buttes gave up the golden California glow of summer and settled back to a brooding, moody sobriety, sometimes retreating pensively behind a smoky veil.

I also was made pensive and expectant by this new autumn and would throw open all the windows of my high room, waiting for whatever winter would be in this new land. Feeling myself to be somehow a child of the place, I waited naturally for permission to cross the boundary between my towering visions, my dizzying dreams of the Mountain, and its actual landscape, the idea of which possessed my helpless and innocent heart.

The permission came with the rains. All through the summer, the vast farmland valley had been soaked in irrigation water and in the orchards and grain fields, the air was thick and humid. Only the island of the Mountain had been dry. When the tentative stage of coming rain passed and it finally poured over the landscape, that whole parched, crunching carpet of desperate, desiccated vegetation, lying like a circular throw-rug over the high volcanic island, exploded in a mixture of fragrance and atmosphere that was almost dizzying. Even from my tower or from my bed beneath open windows, I could smell the Buttes after the first rain and my head would swim with a feeling of painful sweetness. So when the land was well soaked and the veins of the mountain filled, the permission came, and the rising winter wind pushed me to the Buttes. I was a naïve and gullible novice and it was to be an astounding initiation.

Half the day had passed before I finally stood within the opening arms of Brockman Canyon. I was stopped in my tracks by a strong, mixed feeling of anticipation and apprehension. I felt this in my stomach. From tower and dreams, I had become deeply familiar with these Buttes as a giant disk of cosmic geography, seen through reverie and distance as a *complete place* well enclosed within a definite circumference. Now that broad vision was lost, and I was confronted with a wall of sharp escarpments dimly seen through mist in the foreground, evaporating into utter formlessness as they melted into the gray sky. The mouth of the canyon, smothered in cloud, seemed to be plugged by a dense forest, piled thickly at its entrance and literally growing out of a fantastic pile of ancient lumber where a 19th-century ranch house had long ago collapsed into an unrecognizable heap. Disheveled lumber and crowded thicket were like a dark doorway to the canyon, and standing before it tightly narrowed the aperture of my vision. I struggled unsuccessfully to picture where I was in that great and beckoning cluster of peaks seen from my tower.

I ducked beneath wet live oak boughs, picked my way through the prostrate and broken house, and slid down the bank of a small, rushing stream. It was as if a conversation I had been having within myself was abruptly hushed by that cascading, roiling, boundless song of water and rock. With no thought now, only the water whispering and singing in my ears, I moved slowly up the stream. The dense riparian corridor, from which I felt a force pushing and pulling me further, was filled with growing things I had never seen. Tall, sharp-leafed bushes dipped branches laden with bright red berries into the steam, bobbing rhythmically up and down. Hanging all around were vines sprinkled with the remnants of small, feathery globes and dried seedpods like small, brown bananas split and open. The streambed was cobbled in polished boulders, gray and lavender. On one side I stopped, fascinated, beside a large flat rock, pierced in its very center with a perfectly round, deep pit. I knew at once that it had been sculpted by ancient hands and I stood for a long time running my fingers around its smoothed circumference.

At first the winter's new grass crowded down to the creek's edge, and somber, dripping oaks crouched over the dim green of the banks.

A few yards further upstream, I came upon a whole assemblage of huge rounded boulders, very broad and much higher than my head, crowded close to the creek and back beneath the spreading live oaks. They were smothered in a blanket of moss so green that it seemed phosphorescent even in the deep shadow. In wonder I approached and pressed my hands, then my face into the soft cushion. Although I knew quite well it was cool and wet, the moss felt inexplicably warm to me. I was attracted to a small cleft between two great mossy shoulders. I crawled into that cleft, sinking into deep wet grass, the big rocks towering over me on both sides. It felt lovely to be so enclosed. The stream's song was only a faint whisper now, and my thoughts returned. Here, only half-mile or so up the canyon, I began to consider whether there was any reason to proceed further. I felt overpoweringly at rest. To have discovered this fairy bower that felt then like some deep heart of the mountain seemed quite enough. I closed my eyes and listened to the whispers around me. I was almost asleep between the cushions of moss, on this bed of tender grass. When I opened my eyes again suddenly it seemed noticeably darker. With a small flash of alarm, I jumped up and again without thought returned to the beckoning pathway of the stream. The idea of stopping there disappeared, and I was possessed of a conviction that I must go on.

A half-mile further through thickening foliage, the stream turned abruptly to the right, where it poured from a deep gorge. There were no grassy banks and mossy boulders here, only nearly vertical walls of weathered, conglomerate rocks seeping water across their face. Ferns, some small and delicate, some large and primeval, grew in multitudes from the tiny rivulets that whispered down into the stream. Here the creek raised its voice, and the liquid booms and loud gurgles told of steep descents and sharply falling water. I paused again. There was no streamside path. In order to proceed, I must walk in the cold churning water and over polished stones. I looked up to oaks clinging to edges high above and saw that the deepening clouds had descended into the treetops, dragging fingers in the steam. Almost in an instant, light, broken mist thickened to fog. The tunnel of the canyon had narrowed even more. I could see only the festooned rocks rising just before me, and the steam, broken and spraying now, issued toward me out of an opaque curtain of cloud.

I had no reference here but the stream itself and could see very little of my surroundings. But knowing that the water's flow would be like a guiding silver thread unraveled into a cavern, I moved slowly forward, stepping and slipping my way from rock to rock. The plunging water now roared within the narrow gorge, and the sound, like the fog, blocked my perceptions and thoughts. Then, suddenly breaking through this dim thickness of sound and air, I stood amazed before a scene I thought must surely be a dream.

The canyon ended in a sheer, concave wall of fern-covered rock, and a waterfall, shifting like strands of silk twisting and turning in its descent, fell twenty feet into a perfect, still pool. A large cottonwood leaned over the pond, festooned with long wild grape vines to which clung a few red, heart-shaped leaves. Some of these floated tranquilly in the water. Just to the side of the waterfall's spray, a large rock, rising from the pool, cupped on its surface like the palm of a hand, held an offering of water endlessly filled by the falls. And there, drinking from that stony palm, stood a large, pure-white deer, antlers spreading, rising like a ghost from still water, so much whiter than the fog that his body glowed in sharp relief against the lambent spray.

With a gasp I was stunned to stillness. I was hidden by vines and the waterfall's roar, and the white deer seemed not to notice me. After drinking deeply, he lifted his head. Diamonds dripped one by one from his chin. I thought he was looking directly at me. Then he slowly swung his antlered head, stepped delicately out of the pool and bounded up the canyon wall, his whiteness blending and blurring with the thickening fog. He was gone, and he left me wondering if I had actually seen him at all.

I wanted to follow him. To me he was as much an avatar of dream as a unicorn. I wanted to approach him, find him tame and wise and kind and wrap my arms around his neck. I splashed across the pond to the basin where he had drunk, touched the water, then scrambled and struggled up the bank in the deepening dark, following the narrow, black slashes in the earth made by the white deer's ascent.

At the top of the climb, the song of the stream was only a whisper rising through the mist. I was in a narrow glade, bare spreading oaks evenly spaced, deep grass carpeting the ground, higher and thicker beneath each tree's canopy. A low stone wall constructed of well-fitted boulders made a border to canyon's edge and curved out of sight in the fog. The white deer's tracks were plainly etched in the grass and I followed them without hesitation. He was running upward, far, far ahead of me, and the slope of the hill quickly steepened. I began to climb. The mountainside, still covered in cloud, revealed itself only step by step. I was breathing heavily. In twenty minutes thickets of manzanita crowded between the oaks. I passed huge, car-sized rocks far above the shelter of the deep canyon and bare of the soft blankets of moss that had seduced me below. Twenty minutes more and the trees fell behind. Chaparral now blocked my way, and I had to fall to my hands and knees and crawl like a rabbit beneath the bushes' sharp, grasping fingers. The white deer's tracks had disappeared. Still crawling on all fours, I pushed myself upward over the steepening terrain. Without warning, I came abruptly against the smooth face of a cliff, disappearing above me into the thick, gray sky. I stood up and moved around to the right, gaining still more elevation.

Purely by chance, I found my feet treading the shallow trough of a narrow path. It seemed to have been made by many small hooves and paws; indeed here and there in soft places, there were indecipherable tracks. The trail swung upward in a grassy splitting of the cliff. I began to notice a most subtle change in the air. Very still below in the canyon, it was now, near the mountaintop, stirring, and I could feel it cold and wet on my face. There was a change in the light too as the fog thinned and dissipated a little. While below there had been no hint of sunglow, here just a suggestion of pink light filtered through moving mist. Seeing nothing above or below, I was surprised to suddenly find myself standing high atop a domed summit, broad and bare except for one fantastically dwarfed and twisted oak growing from a crack in solid rock.

Below and before me stretched a sloping expanse of chaparral so thick the ground beneath it could not be seen. Here on this summit, the cloud that lay heavily on the landscape below was broken and drifting, revealing patches of a high, wild terrain. Once again, as below I had snuggled in the moss, I felt here deeply content and satisfied in this place. The broad summit seemed to be my destination. I felt that I had gone far enough. The low sky concealed from me any conception of the Buttes' extent and complexity. I could see that it was nearly dark. Now, from the tower behind the house, I had looked westward and obsessively pondered this unearthly island of pinnacles floating in the farmland sea, and my soul, slipping its moorings, often drifted into strange and unknown regions of spirit. But there on the tower, if I simply swiveled my head around, I could see my house; indeed, the very windows of my room where I slept in a bed fragrant with a mother's care, and could sometimes hear the chatter and laughter of my family and my father's voice leading hymns around the piano. I was only a child after all, and balancing on a rock, alone at the very verge of this gray, misty void, I suddenly felt a pang of fear and the longing for a return to the proper world of a child. I began to turn about to retrace my long journey.

Then out of the corner of my eye, I caught a flash of white below. Focusing my gaze, I saw, unmistakably, the white buck bounding across that thicket. In a very small clearing he stopped, seemed to look back, then flicked with amazing speed around the edge of the next peak beyond the tangled declivity. It was true that this moonscape in the cold, failing light where I felt now I had foolishly overstayed my welcome, filled me with thoughts of Mother, fireside and bed. But the white deer, instantly more familiar and compelling than any human parent and any domestic sanctuary, caused me to utterly forget the world below. Thoughts of return were swept from my mind, and I spontaneously followed the deer, descending into the chaparral and hurriedly threading my way toward that adjacent peak that rose sharply from the halo of brush. It had the form of a high castle's turret, and reaching its base, I began to climb.

I was rather stunned by the force and sharpness of the jagged, bristling shards that towered above me as I neared the summit. The rocks were massive and cold and deeply cloven with crevices that, in the failing light, seemed bottomless and black. I found it difficult to move forward without getting tangled in thick and grasping foliage, piled in between the towering sections of the cliffs. The fog had moved in behind and around me again, and even if my attention had been turned toward the wider horizon, I could not have seen fifty feet in any direction. Moisture hung heavily in the leaves. I was overwhelmed then with the pungent, intense odor of bay laurel, its evergreen, narrow-leafed branches and smooth trunks crowding all around me in the narrow gaps between towering monoliths. Even now, a life-time later, a chance encounter with that wonderful bouquet anywhere will paralyze me with the presence and awareness of those high cliffs of the Buttes and my introduction to this ancient realm of dream.

Cold as were the rocks around me, their familiar solidity drew me closely to them. They seemed deeply comforting and I pressed my body against them, feeling anchored in a profound and mystic way. I was aware then that I loved the sensation of that crystalline surface on my face and hands. Almost at the very pinnacle, I came suddenly upon an enclosed and tunneled cleft between two standing shards. It presented a dark hallway with a glimmer of evening light coming through the other end. I squeezed in, crawling along the sandy floor. I was completely enclosed.

I have no idea how many minutes I lay on my stomach in that long, hall-like crack, my chin over the threshold of its outer door, the black silhouette of the walls around me, the deepening darkness of the Buttes' unknown, inner landscape below. In light barely adequate for sight, I saw colonnades of spires looming on all sides. I saw canyons like jagged cuts in the mountainsides plunging down around me and etched between neighboring peaks. I felt the moan of air moving, not wind really, just masses of invisible air booming far below the range of human hearing. I heard water rushing in unseen cascades, and I heard its echo on the stone walls around me. I heard also the thin, distant piping of geese somewhere up there in the impenetrable gray over the peaks, and for an instant I had a vision, detailed like a picture etched in glass, of the whole circular mass of volcanoes from high, high above, reaching toward the unseen stars, up out of the blackness of the valley.

Hypnotized and seduced by that soaring dream, when I finally awoke and scooted out of the little cliff-edged cave back onto the more level surface near the summit, my sense of direction had been completely neutralized, although I was entirely unaware of this at the time. While I had been utterly preoccupied with the enclosure and the strange trance it had induced, the fog had swept inward and upward thickly and enveloped the whole of my surroundings. I was absolutely, frighteningly alone. I had been tricked by the comfort of that rock close about me and now an incredible dark landscape as strange as the moon stretched all around me. Without my even marking the time, the night had fallen. But I knew I had climbed here from a canyon far below, and before me a huge, broad canyon dropped into blackness. Downward and across this chasm was, I thought most confidently, the way I had come. The stream was below, flowing downward and outward to the south, and surely, following slope and water, I could not help but arrive on the road leading east to the tall old house.

But I was as utterly fooled as I could possibly have been. I had entered the circular wilderness of the Buttes from their southern edge and penetrated northward only about three miles into their confused, indecipherable diameter, a diameter ten miles in a straight line, but stretching up and down and back and forth for many more. By now it was black as pitch and I could not see an oak ten feet before my face, much less any guiding landmark. Yet my foolish directional intuition, which I always thought I had inherited from my farmer father, remained intact. With all of my senses unthinkingly confident of my southerly direction, I was in fact heading, in the dark, due north directly toward unknown miles and miles of cliff, chasm and canyon, into a night most black, foggy and impenetrable. Thus had the Mountain arranged my first, trusting surrender.

From tower, bedroom window and soaring dreams I had felt the force of this whole, spinning, volcanic cosmos rising from the vast valley. Now here, deep in the dark night of the place itself, I could feel only handfuls of the very soil I grasped as I began to slide down the steep and black decline. I had at once an expectation of a familiar arrival, and a disquieting sense that this slope seemed much steeper than the one I had ascended in pursuit of the white deer. No matter. Sense of steepness was a subtle thing no doubt influenced by fear, darkness, unfamiliarity and a muddy footing. I really was unable to stand upright as I slid downward. I leaned into the slope, my face brushing wet grass unseen, fingers grasping whatever rocks they found. Suddenly, soft slope failed me and I dropped. There was only time for a flash of fear before my feet sunk in the soil again. Fifty feet more and this surprise was repeated. I seemed to be descending a series of terraces divided by small cliffs, like the sides of an amphitheater. As I continued, the thought of a deeper, more dangerous cliff crossed my mind, but I knew I had encountered no such precipice on my way up, so I felt relatively safe. I increased my sliding speed, anxious to arrive at the bottom. I suppose a half-hour passed in this way. Finally I felt the ground level beneath me, and felt also a resurgence of confidence, trust really, in this mysterious landscape, unknown yet loved.

    I had dropped rapidly back to canyon bottom, and I had plunged also into the very thickest of fog, lying like a damp, gray blanket all around me. I strained to hear the whispering of the creek, but sound was smothered. I lifted my hand and brought it before my face. I could see only the dimmest outline of my spreading fingers. Now, like one blind, I reached both arms before me and began to step very slowly forward. Almost at once I came up against the trunk of a tree. I felt satisfied to recognize the deeply etched bark of a Valley Oak, like the ones in my yard at home. I went carefully on, now stepping around a tree, now stumbling a little on a tuft of grass or a scattered rock, although the terrain here seemed generally soft and gentle beneath my feet. With each step I expected the glade, where I had seen the rock wall earlier, to end. I expected to find the waterfall and then the stream, to lead me faithfully out of the canyon. That familiarity never came. In the deep darkness I slowly ventured step after step, for what seemed at least a hundred yards. I was walking in a black void.

Without warning from any of my senses, my outstretched palms struck against a flat, board wall. It was rough and even splintery, reminiscent of the old outbuildings around my house. A sense of deep confusion came upon me. I ran my hands along the boards to the left until the structure, whatever it was, ended in just a few feet. Then I moved to the right and in only several steps felt the pliancy of an unhinged door. There were muffled creaks as I pushed it open. Like a ghost rushing out and into my face, odors of nesting owls, dry wood and old ashes swept past me. Inside, sheltered now, I no longer felt the mist upon my face. In fact I could hear, just faintly, a dripping on the roof. My knees struck something hard and angular. I grasped what I recognized as an iron bed-rail. Sinking to my knees, I explored the shape of a small cot, spring net suspended on a narrow frame. In mind's eye I saw it rusty and ancient, decorated with cobwebs. Just next to the bed I could see something black and bulky. Touch revealed a woodstove, grimy, exhaling the breath of ashes.

I knew quite well now that I had somehow strayed far off my course home. I no long understood clearly the connection between where I was here in this black mountain and where I had been, in my orchards, in my yard, in my tower and my room. The pathway between these worlds had been erased from me. Thus severed as I was, I clutched at the possibility of simply staying here in this old cabin, simply waiting until daylight before going on. But I had been still long enough to feel really chilled and damp. Any imaginary sense of warmth and shelter drained away. I felt suddenly as if I had been tricked and caught, but I told myself, "It'll be alright. I just started down too far east or west. If I keep going I've got to come to the road sooner or later. That is better than sitting here all night."

So under this fresh delusion, I stumbled back out into the wet night. Immediately behind the old cabin, trees and brush thickened. I was in a hurry now, and pushed my way through. The rushing of water swelled suddenly around me. But I was not encouraged, for this stream flowed not through a narrow canyon, but obviously even in the dark, across a broad flat. This creek seemed very wide. It was much too dark to pick a way across on stones or cobbles. I did not hesitate to step into the stream. Immediately I stumbled and fell onto my hands and knees. Cold water struck my stomach. Gasping in shock, I scrambled out to the other side. Wrapping my arms around my face, I pushed on through sharp, resistant branches.

Then again there were rocks and slippery earth and a sharp rising of the ground as steep as a stairway.

Now I was completely stunned. The landscape over which I had come flashed in bright pictures behind my eyes. Flat orchard and road leading west from my house to the Buttes; low rampart hills sinking behind me where the mountains ended to the south; Brockman Canyon slicing into the pinnacled wilderness to the north, its stream pouring out to me where I had stood ready to enter; the white deer in his deep canyon luring me upward to a first and single summit. All of this revealed to me in a flash that to have encountered another canyon wall here meant only one thing. "Somehow I started down in some other direction far, far away from the waterfall."

And yet so powerfully and completely had my sense of direction been turned inside-out by that reverie in the rock, so surely had I felt my southerly direction when I had started down toward the road, that all of these anomalies and confusions were neutralized and reshaped into a fundamental presumption that if I just kept going my expectations would be fulfilled.

So now I began to climb even deeper into this dream of sightless sense and mystery. The smell of this place was on my face, in my nostrils. My clothes were wet, and the feeling of the Mountain's water seemed almost under my skin. There was a choir of sound; rain, wind, birdcall, so many infinitesimal voices, like strands of tangled music that sounded equally inside and outside my head and dissolved the boundaries of my hearing. As I climbed on, my body felt stretched across not only its short length of steep hillside, but stretched also like a vast cloud over all this landscape. It was then that I began to know a perception that would follow my life: the swells and angles and features of my body were the swales and contours of the Mountain, the shape of the Mountains' skin. I was here in the shape of a small boy, and here also in the form of a mountain. This was not understood in words or even ideas. It was felt, I think now, in the way an infant feels the body of a parent. And clinging to that precipitous, unexpected incline in the dark, creeping upward like a lizard prone and close to the dirt, all my fear left me. My towering vision of the volcanic island's circle, spinning between earth and sky, and this small, precious piece of the place holding tightly to my body, merged into one sense of being. It was as if I were consuming mouthfuls of the place, swallowing it into the pit of my stomach, drawing it into the cavern of my heart.

But I was still, indeed, climbing an ever-steepening mountainside in almost complete darkness, and if I was now without fear, I was not without caution. These many peaks clustered together had the shapes of old volcanoes after all, and this one I now climbed in the dark, like many others, rose like a forested cone for a thousand feet before its rounded, upward slopes were pierced by huge, almost vertical monoliths reaching upward hundreds of feet higher. I was exhausted, and again I rested for a moment in the sandy crease at the margin of grassy hillside and crystalline spire, behind a fragrant fence of bay.

I was not thinking any longer about my choices, not considering my route in any rational way. Truly, my judgment, certainly already limited by my age, was now quite smothered by this ecstatic landscape. I was going to climb the cliff and go right over the very top of this mountain. When I stood up and reached for the rock, I felt at once a deep crevice stuffed with grass and short brush, like the chinking between upright logs. Up I climbed. It felt somewhat like going up a ladder. Wherever I reached, I found some kind of hold. I sensed full well the abyss behind me, but there was a thinning of the air here that encouraged me, a softening of the fog. Now I felt a breath of breeze on my face. Crevices and grass and brush had ended. My toes quivered, supporting me on a very small ledge, my hands tightly gripping the rough and broken surface above me. I had climbed very high and hung like a little bat upon a rock-face I could barely see.

But now there was no longer a way directly up. Here as I reached above my head, I found the cliff's surface very smooth, almost sandy. I craned my neck to my right and stared hard into the wet blackness. There was a shifting of the mist, and something like light—the glow of high stars—glittered for an instant beyond me. In that instant, I saw that the crack my toes were wedged into ran away from me, upward at a shallow angle along the cliff-face. Without knowing where it led, I inched myself around until my back was against the rock. Slowly kneeling so that my heels hung onto the crevice and my flattened hands pressed against stone behind me, I began to inch sideways. That vagrant starlight vanished. With the strain of my crab-like movement I closed my eyes tightly, just feeling, feeling my way as I crept inch by inch along the cliff.

Without any warning the crevice ran out. My heels began to slip. My hands scraped against the cliff as I, oh so very slowly, began to slide downward toward an inky depth. This was a feeling that had no doubt been one of the last for many a doomed climber elsewhere, but that is not what happened to me. It never occurred to me that I would fall, perhaps because I could not see below my feet in the foggy gloom, perhaps because I was simply filled with an absolute and naïve trust. But I came to rest upon a very soft bed of winter grass.

I had fallen gently off the lip of the cliff and into the mouth of a dry, sandy-floored cave. Behind me the air was empty, moist, ringing and echoing with depth and vastness, and cold, stirring wind. But before me, inside the cave, was completely still, warm, dry air and an enclosing, curving hand of stone, pressing close around me. Now I felt the mountain swallowing *me*.

Crawling to the back of the cave, I came upon a pile of dry twigs and branches, and touching them brought a vision of a bright, crackling fire. But it was not actually as dry inside as it had seemed in contrast to the wet night, and my damp and muddy pockets held no matches. There was no chance for a fire and I dismissed it from my mind. Instead, I lay down on the sandy floor and stared into darkness, letting myself feel the restful pressure of stone all around me. Of all places I had seen and felt on this wandering initiation, in faint daylight and darkness, this cave held me most powerfully. I remembered it from my dreams. I had no doubt whatsoever that I would spend many days and nights of my life there. Again my fatigue and the comfort of enclosure made me think of remaining where I was, of going no further until dawn. But I had no clear sense of how late into the night and the mountain I had ventured. I felt I was very close to the pinnacle. I imagined myself having a clear, revealing view at the top and reasserting my course to the road and home.

So I left the cave and plunged back into blind vastness, pulling myself upward, further and further. Overcome with fatigue, I dropped to my knees to rest in what seemed a very small alcove on the cliff. I noticed here immediately a spicy, pungent scent, and feeling intuitively that it was a plant or shrub of some kind, I reached out blindly in the dark. My hands rubbed against a broad, twisted, very rough surface. Wrapping my arms around it, I could feel that I was embracing the bole of a thick tree. Its shape and actual size were unknowable in the blackness, and I could tell nothing of what sort of tree it really was. I knew it was not an oak. Absent was the sensual, smooth skin of the manazita. Its overwhelming acidic scent was hypnotic. Its rough trunk felt somehow warm in the wet night and I was reluctant to leave the alcove. But I knew I must move forward and upward, so I tore myself away from this comforting spot and scrambled rapidly over sharp rocks above. A final step, and I suddenly seemed to be floating, riding on a flat disk of rock, sparkling beneath my feet in the shocking glow of an unguessed moon. I had passed through the cloud and come to the very summit where I knew I was standing on a two-thousand foot tower above the floor of the great valley, where distance would collapse and sight would be without limit. But all around the circumference of the world, all around beneath the infinite dome of the night sky, a blanket of fog, like snow or billowed cotton, reflecting the moon, covered everything. Nothing could be seen below. Only three peaks of this Middle Mountain rose above, floating on the clouds beneath the moon, and I, alone, was at the very star-touching pinnacle of one.

But although I could see into the heavens from this high place, I could see nothing whatever of the landscape over which

I had crawled, nothing of the valley lights that I knew sparkled somewhere below the fog. I felt convinced now that although I had not started back in a directly southerly direction, my steps had trended in the dark sharply toward the southeast, and that instead of returning to the east-west road straight away, I must be feeling my way almost parallel to it. But still, if I continued, I would most certainly strike that road eventually.

So I left the peak and the moon and the stars and plunged again into the soft, black cloud. The mist was so heavy that moisture collected on my face like raindrops. I was very wet, and to be still was uncomfortable. It was much better to move. Everything now seemed downhill. I had the sense of being poured from a dipping hand. Oak forest was dense, and I still had to walk slowly, both hands stretched out before me, to avoid collisions in the wet dark. But the downhill terrain seemed calmer and gentler. Occasionally, I would stumble at the sudden drop of a small gully, and had to continue on my hands and knees for awhile. The fog was thinning as I went down hill, and although the sky was absolutely black and opaque, I began to see a little of dark, looming forms around me, and flat expanses that seemed to glow very dimly. Suddenly I heard the piping of high geese again, and this sound was followed by a rasping, funereal wail in a minor note, a descending release of unearthly tones, the voice of owls familiar to me from the moonlit yard at home. I had the unreasonable thought that somehow the same birds had found me here in the Mountain's black night. There was the whisper of a breeze all around that seemed to softly hiss along the outside of a bubble, a membranous sphere in which I walked hypnotically. I passed now into a sort of pacing trance, on and on. I think another hour or two must have passed. I became aware that I had dropped into another small valley enclosed by hills. There was tall grass nearly to my waist. I heard suddenly the soft note of a bell, and several murky shapes whispered through the grass ahead of me. I recognized them as sheep and I thought of soft wool and gentle eyes. Home was ahead. I wanted to be warm and dry and to sleep.

While I had been carried by a strange destiny and my parents' dreams to the foot of an earth-form that had possessed my soul; while I floated like an embryo in the womb of a very small enclosing world, the specter of atomic holocaust terrorized the wider life of the times. Cold War. I had never heard the term, but the Buttes, commonplace and taken for granted by the valley's population, viscerally divine and infinite to me, were for a time a launching pad for unimaginable and potential destruction. Three Titan missile bases had been built in northern California, and one had been hidden deep in the ground at the very northern edge of the Buttes where the last hints of the hill faded into the flat expanse of farmland. Here, a chasm the size of a football field and as deep as an open-pit mine had been gouged in the volcanic sediments. Within it had been constructed a concrete structure shaped like a huge bicycle wheel with a few great, thick spokes. At the end of these spoke-like tunnels, three nuclear warheads waited atop their rockets for someone to pull the atomic trigger. After construction, the whole complex had been completely reburied under the soil and gravel of the excavation, and there below the earth dozens of people scurried about their duties like ants in their burrow, maintaining an absolute maze of wire, electronics and lethally volatile fuel. But on the surface, beneath the night sky, there were to be seen only an asphalt road, a high fence, a small guard booth, and a blazing floodlight on a high pole.

And so I padded down the last gentle hill. I knew that dawn was near, both from the sense of a whole night passed walking and crawling in the dark and from what was a subliminal hint of light along a vague horizon. Still, night prevailed above. "The road will be here pretty soon," I said to myself. "I must have come out half-way back to town." Then, as I passed through a thicket of small oaks, a blazing light struck my face, blinding me more completely than the dark. After at least ten hours in complete darkness, it hurt my eyes. I stood like a statue, arms limply at my sides. My brain stopped and I settled shakily down in the grass. "It must be something in town…like a baseball field or a parking lot or something," I murmured. I began to walk again. Now I saw the fence and behind it the guardhouse and I began to discern the floodlight atop its pole. I had seen the missile base once from a car window, and I suppose I finally knew where I had emerged from the great circle of jagged upland that was the Buttes. But I began to cry now for the first time in all that dark, wet, stumbling, ecstatic journey through all that long night. I cried at having been absolutely confounded. I cried with the confusion of south having incomprehensibly become north. I cried because this place I loved so much for the power and energy it had poured into me had now exhausted me and turned the world inside out.

Two young sentries in the guardhouse eventually noticed the figure of a small boy clinging to the fence, dripping and smeared with mud. There were phone calls to an Air Force base, sheriff's office and sleepless parents. There was a tense, silent ride home with my father in the thin dawn. There was a warm bath and a sinking into dream in the huge four-poster bed beneath the open windows of my room where the Valley Oaks whispered in the breeze of a clear morning. And far away across the tattered winter fields, the sharp sunlight of a cold, crystal day flooded all the secret crevices of the Buttes where I had crept with darkened eye and quickened soul.

As spring followed winter and summer followed spring, I retraced those dark steps of that first initiation many, many times. I learned to know by many paths the way to the waterfall. I had other glimpses of white deer and knew he had not been only a spirit. I sat for many long hours in that trickster crevice and contemplated how I had become lost, like a child blindfolded, spun around and set to wander mistakenly. Seeing the cliffs in daylight I remained completely mystified by how I had climbed them in the dark. I poked my way up and down the volcanic terraces of Braggs Canyon, sat for long hours in the tiny brown cabin before its cold ashen stove. I did light many small, bright fires in that sweet cave, where in the daylight I found a collection of antlers bleached white with age, scattered inside. I handled often an old frying pan and some coffee tins from an antique era that had been hidden beneath some blackened stones by someone I did not know but felt near me. The last, little valley with the tall grass and shuffling sheep, became as much a home for me as my parents' house. As boyhood birthdays passed, I learned all of this landscape, east to west, north to south, so very well that I could bring it all to bright actuality in my mind and walk there while lying in my bed.

Yet it was not by sight that I had actually learned the Buttes. During that first night, I had crawled over the entire circular landscape, south to north, and I learned it then by the sensation of its rock and soil on my body, the rising and falling of its contour beneath my hands and feet and knees, the pungent scent of its wet moss, brewing soil, and ripening fruit, the sound of its winds, waters, and creatures around my ears in the blackness. The Place *in its totality* was imprinted on some hidden surface of my subconscious, so that I never ceased to feel the Buttes as part of my own body. And this knowledge of the place, intuitive in me thereafter, always underlay all of my subsequent visual experience there.

Something else had been imprinted during that night as well; a wordless conviction that I knew the Mountain utterly and yet knew it utterly not at all; and that this paradox equally and concurrently pervaded my own individual being. From that time on, with every step I took there, with every warm cave and wet, green canyon and serrated ridge or peak I explored, a sense of inexplicable mystery grew in me, even as the Mountain's voice endlessly whispered, "Although your path is a mystery indeed, still the beginning and the ending of everything for you, is here."

III

Forgive me for this flight I now take you on into a region of deep and tender intimacy and private tragedy. But I can think of no better way of unfolding to you how this place, this figure of the earth, was the hall and temple of the highest and most lovely, as well as the deepest and darkest extensions of my humanity; and without showing you this I cannot show you what sort of place this small volcanic island really is, and how such a place can act upon the life of a human being.

I was fifteen and not nearly seasoned enough for what was to come. But some quality of my childhood had been vandalized by the power of this mountain. The imperious force of its personality, the inexorableness of its being, had pressed me to such a thinness of spirit, such a transparency of existence, that the great fires pervasive for human beings in the universe burned through me and gleamed in my eyes in ways fifteen-year-olds are not really meant to see.

How strange it was then that so boundless, so primeval a passion as the one that was to come, should come to me within such a heavily bounded space: the pale plastered plainness of a country Christian church. But so it was. I sat stiffly in the pew, pressed close to my mother by our fellow parishioners and my little siblings. My father was in the pulpit that day, delivering a sermon in place of the absent pastor. I remember he was speaking about working on earth while waiting on the Lord's coming, and he had a quaver in his voice and a misty eye as he said, "When that cloud the size of a man's hand appears, the celestial glory of the returning Christ which will erase all our works and make all things new, I pray that he find me not idly waiting, but with a hammer in my hand, uplifted in the performance of his work on earth."

It was at that moment that she slipped from the periphery of my vision from some place I could not even guess, into my full view. She was a slender, long-waisted girl, a couple of years older than me, flaming auburn hair about her shoulders, large gazing eyes above fine bold lips, a complexion of cream. She wore a sort of knitted dress, full below the waist in colored pleats, bodice of black closely embracing her form above. A scent touched me as she passed, and she and her family, arriving late, settled just far enough ahead and to one side so that she was all I could see and an unprecedented rushing in my soul was all that I could hear.

Most Sabbath mornings as I sat in the milky light of that little church and the pastor's voice droned away over Daniel and the Revelation, Justification by Works or Faith, The Second Coming or the Meaning of the Sabbath, my spirit was away hovering like a fledgling falcon over the Buttes, sailing down misty canyons, peering into caves as I passed, or clinging to star-sprinkled pinnacles. Church I recognized and respected as a place where the profane was suspended and the sacred inhaled, and this I did with religious zeal, although the nature of my worship would have dismayed the pastor and my parents. This Sabbath while I spun in the dizziness of her presence, I worshipped so still. But now the sacred inhaled was that scent she left as she passed. Throughout the service, I sank deeper and deeper into her strange but utterly familiar being. I watched the barely perceptible motions of her face as her eye flickered about the assembly. I watched her shoulders and her breast rise and fall as she breathed. I knew nothing of her but her form and its subtle motion, but on that Sabbath morning I fell deeply and desperately in love with her.

When, on the way home in the station wagon I heard my mother say these new arrivals were coming for dinner, I was numb with terror. Dashing to my room, my first thought was to run away to the Buttes, as I always did on Sabbath afternoons, to continue my worship. This day it was not worship I wanted, but safety, invisibility, that matchless soft solitude I found only in that Place, where all that was real and without doubt in me was all that I could see.

I was sitting on the edge of the ancient four-poster bed I had inherited from the old house, gazing through the oak leaves outside my western wall of windows, my eyes fixed on the volcanic form that defined my world, when I heard her voice in the garden below. She was laughing and speaking at once, answering some inquiry from my parents who were welcoming her family to our house. There was a wild sort of extravagance to her manner of speaking, a sort of gushing sweetness, a forceful soft babbling that I learned later was colored with the intonation of northern California's tiny logging towns where her father worked and where she had grown from tomboy childhood to this frightening, girlhood beauty. They rounded the back of the house and approached the walk directly below me. I leaned forward and looked down. Her voice was still running on, but even as she spoke and I stole a glance downward, she peered directly upward through the trees. Her large eyes were opened very wide, deer-like as she looked upward to my window, and she pinned me like a moth with her glance. She caught my eye and there was just the faintest, most rapid flicker of a smile that I could see before I fell back upon my bed, my heart pounding. The door slammed and they were inside the house downstairs.

I was thinking hard about slipping out of the window over the back porch roof and escaping down the vent pipe and into the country-side when my mother called me to dinner from the hall below. I crept down the stairs, and without looking up or around, slid into the dining room, slid into my chair, and slid into a thick protective silence while everyone else chattered happily while they ate.

Her name was *Avalee*, a sound hauntingly beautiful to me still, even as she was herself. She was eighteen and was finishing her senior high school year at home while her father finished his work at a mill in town. She liked Christian music and she sang, she said, in answer to my father, who was our family purveyor of devotional hymns. She passionately loved horses and had ridden rough mountain trails all her life. She was unused to the dull flatness of the Sacramento Valley and was going to miss the mountains.

Then, although she had been exchanging remarks with nearly everyone at our table except me, she asked me a direct question. What about those funny little hills that poked up nearby, those *Buttes*? She said the word with a touch of sarcasm. It sounded a little like a playful taunt. Perhaps someone in my family had been profiling me in my absence and had mentioned my obsession with the Buttes. Perhaps she had surmised, in the crafty penetrating way she had, that I would be the person who must know. I had no idea at the time why she had directed her question about the Place at me, but if she had suddenly inquired of me why I had fallen so desperately in love with her that morning in church, she could not have stepped more assuredly into the most intimate and passionate chamber of my heart.

My ears were burning painfully. "Well, I'm going out there right after dinner," I murmured.

"Good!" she cried triumphantly. "I'll go with you!"

It had rained that morning, one of those sudden, late October showers that pat the dry hills of the Buttes with soft moist hands. Clouds of scent rose into the air; ripe grass, tarweed, thistle and dust, mixed in rainy mist. I was dizzy with the scent of the rain and the scent of the girl. Fall-brown hillsides, their color deepened by the rain seemed swept by the wind upslope to the high rocks. There was no clear division between the peaks and the sky above. Both lines were merged and mixed.

It was a somber Sabbath afternoon in the Buttes, the kind I loved the best. Alone, I would have drunk in the sadness of that gray landscape. I would have been swimming in the mist of its sweet melancholy, for joy and sadness were always flowing from the peaks through me alternately. But today Avalee filled everything. Her laughter and chatter rang in my ears. It was difficult for me to attend to the teasing questions she darted at me incessantly. I hopped over a rock wall and turned to help her. She was already nearly over, skillfully balancing on top when she noticed I had extended my hands lamely toward her in a gesture of assistance she did not need. For an instant she delayed her progress, took my hands and somehow skillfully guided my grasp to her waist. I can never forget the sensation of my hands seeming almost to meet around her. She jumped from the rock wall, and for a moment of lovely motion, we spun together beneath the October sky. When her feet lit upon the ground she was gazing fully into my face, and her features were pressed into me, mixed and merged with the features of Brockman Canyon, its arms opening behind and beyond us.

That day I showed her the waterfall that seemed to me like her: slender and flowing, noisy and musical, all of its motion and energy caught and stilled in a dark pool in the canyon's deep shadows. I told her the story of the white deer in the fog, "...standing right there," I said, "sipping water from that little dish on this rock." She touched the place where the white deer's mouth had been. We climbed out of the ferns and wetness and I led her upward toward the place no human being had ever been with me before, a very secret place, my first cave high in the rocks. Filling my mind was an image of the two of us, sitting side by side before my ring of fire rocks while I confessed to her the strange, private glories of my nights there alone. I wanted to take her there, I *yearned* to take her there, but with each step upward my heart pounded with an incomprehensible dread. At the last moment, high on a ridge before another step would take us around a vertical cliff and into full view of the cave's mouth, I lost my courage and turned back another way, and we stood on the edge of the abyss. I was inexpressibly somber and melancholy and she teased me and chided me playfully.

Seated on the cliff's edge, we watched in silence as fog rolled up the Sacramento River and tumbled into the canyons far below our high perspective. By some silent cue, we rose and began walking down and south. I felt strangely struck down by my failure to take her to the most intimate place I knew, but feverish and agitated in some new way. She was serious and silent for the first time that day. I had guided her through the veil, from that outer world into the fairy one of my own, where no one quite knew the way but me. I was frightened as if there might be some danger in having taken her so close to that place. I wanted agonizingly to take her hand in the fading light, but she marched assertively along just out of reach. Back at home, I led her upstairs to show her my room. She put her hand on my bed. She looked wistfully out of my western window at the Buttes' silhouette, sharply visible in a clearing, twilight sky.

For five years I had drifted through these tight, embracing mountains in a dream, my body and my connection to the earth into which it had been born, stretched to a thread-like thinness by the Mountain's unyielding pull on my soul. Just my thoughts turning toward the Place would suddenly make of me something almost transparent and membranous, floating like a kite of fragile tissue, tugging in the wind at a tenuous line.

Since that first morning atop the old water tower behind the house, I had been pulled very suddenly away from thoughtless childhood. Surely it *was* an earth-like landscape that had captured me; grass like water, woodland touching and holding me with a thousand rough and gentle arms, streams flowing over it all and through me like blood. But it had not been a place actually attached to the earth. As a child during those years, in going to the Buttes I had hopped aboard, and the whole volcanic circle, stooping down from the sky to receive me, sailed away, a free-floating island in a cosmos of spirit. And my body became like a ghost there, a nearly invisible shadow that I fancied only the deer and the owls could see. I was not a child of the earth then, not a child of the body.

But now this girl had come into my life and I was suddenly and violently human once again. Somehow her presence and the Mountain had become intermingled. I turned toward that place of spirit as I had always done, but flowing out of it now was this sweet, terrible, human longing. And although it was a simple longing for a slender girl of eighteen whose name was Avalee, it took the dimensions of that immense and overwhelming landscape. The Mountain became soaked in it, huge, heavy, pressing me down to the earth with the warm weight of sweet passion, a new sense of being a human person in a physical world. I felt connected by this new love not only to the peaks and canyons of the place, which were the garden-set stage for the drama of passion unfolding in me, but connected as well to the vast family of my species whose blood I felt flowing through me now. And all of this through the warm being of this young girl I had barely touched and hardly knew.

Perhaps I would have survived then as a youthful spirit if she had disappeared suddenly from me, but I had no doubt that my life on the earth depended absolutely on our loving each other. As the quiet and ambivalent autumn dissolved into winter, my whole soul wept with a yearning that flowed over and through me like rains washing the dark canyons where I now moaned and drifted with the wet December wind.

I had a ritual now that I performed with regularity as the winter bore down on the Sacramento Valley. It was done in two parts. First, on weekends, almost always Sabbaths, I would be pacing in the yard under the huge Valley Oaks, hiding in the jungle-like foliage that ringed the house, or clinging to the top of the tower, looking toward the road and awaiting her arrival. She would come suddenly, laughing and teasing and the cold wind would rise and blow us out across the naked orchards, over soaked and barren fields and into the Buttes. I would walk with her in a state of suspended expectation, feeling the force of my love beating against the inside of my body like a bird violent in a cage.

Going across the open meadows where the new winter green pressed upward beneath the dry carpet of last year's grass, Avalee would always be running ahead, scrambling over fences, balancing atop the rock walls slippery with winter moss. She chattered happily while I gulped and held my breath and exulted whenever I was close to her. Entering the tree-filled canyons, she would become quiet and stand listening to the water murmuring from the green shadows. I was only 15 and she was older but she seemed like a beautiful child to me, always expectant, hushed or exuberant at a moment's passing. All that winter we never touched with intent, except to scramble over rocks together or help each other across the streams. But there was something about these deep mossy places in the Buttes where winter's water tumbled along in stream beds of sculpted lava that made us often stop and stand near each other in silence. It felt to me then as if our hands were touching, as if I were holding her by her fingertips. I deeply wondered if she felt the same. But the soft silence would be suddenly broken by a murmur or a laugh from her and she would run away, not even looking back.

At the apex of those winter days together, we would always emerge from the canyons and climb breathlessly up the peaks to sharp towers of rock alone in the cold sky. There we would stand, our bodies unsteady in the buffeting wind. I would turn toward her, but it seemed she didn't notice, so childishly transfixed she would be by the vastness of the world below and our stunning, high centrality to it all. I could gaze at her then, her auburn hair writhing around her large eyes, her lips slightly parted, inhaling the wind. Her form would be painted against that fantastic landscape, her arms outstretched like wings, her hands open and seeming to grasp the tops of the Blue Oaks below us. At those moments I would hear myself reciting the proclamation of my love, strongly above the whistle of the wind as I imagined it would be. But it was never said, I thought because she would always start into movement just at the moment I was about to speak, dart a teasing glance at me and dash off the rocks and down the hill. My firm intention to confess was only imagined, of course. Whatever she had done, stand still or run, turn toward me or look away, I never could have spoken. I was paralyzed and speechless as we rambled downward and away, until the next unrequited rendezvous would come.

That was the first part of the ritual. The second I would perform alone. Usually as the day began to wane and a wet storm or a soaking winter fog was blowing in, I would reach under my old dresser and remove my "mountain bundle": soft leather moccasins, old brown corduroys and a voluminous green flannel shirt. Not wanting my departure to be seen by anyone I would softly open my window. A rush of wet winter air would engulf me and pull me out onto the roof, down the vent-pipe and away over the fields. Now those arms of the mountain would reach toward me, visibly yearning for me, taking me in, pulling me through the veils, over the rocks, across the streams, through the deep wet grass, back to that dark, soft, green place between the moss-covered boulders, beneath the leaning live-oaks, their thick leaves heavy and drooping over me. There I would sit for a moment inhaling the scent of wet leaves and moss, running my hands through the grass and then over my face. Then quietly, alone and hidden in that deep place, I would weep and pray. I would tell the Father of the Mountain what was happening to me, tell Him of the glory and purity of my love for her, and I would beg for what seemed unthinkable except through His doing—for the sweet completeness of a union of hearts I did not even understand. My voice would rise and fall with the wind and the rain and the brook flowing near my knees.

What a child I was! It was passionate longing in sweet innocence, deep, delicious, yearning love with no understanding and no boundaries. And it continued like this, these Middle Mountain rituals of agonizing, tentative expectation and painful, sweet supplication, all through the wet gray months of that winter.

And like a child aching to reveal some private accomplishment to his parents, I waited breathlessly to show Avalee the coming of spring to the Buttes.

Spring in this island of rocks and water comes like the excess of adolescence. Each year since my arrival, I had felt a vague sense of hesitation as spring approached. I was always reluctant to let go of winter. Those cold sweet rains, pure and exhilarating as they streamed over and through the precious landscape, seemed to flow through my veins. I surged with energy from the winter storms, rambled through the wet and heavy grass, closing my eyes and swirling in the eddies of the creeks, clinging to the high rocks and laughing into the damp wind. I was nourished by the winter weather, and I clung to the soil and rocks and branches of the place like a little frog, so completely was I at home there in winter.

Then in early March, the rains would become less frequent, the clouds white, glowing and purely ornamental. Gentle warm breezes from the north began to dry the soaked landscape. Everything exploded in a riot of bloom. Grass, tentative and carpet-like during winter, seemed pulled up by the sky into a thick green matte. Wildflowers burst open everywhere. But even in the midst of my wonder at the overwhelming beauty of it all I would become aware of a disquieting sensation. It was a faint sense of resentment. I did not really know why. That gray, austere winter purity gradually drained out of the place, evaporating like a dream into the dense blue air of spring. And although just a boy, my soul was harkening to the deep secret of the Mountain, whispered under the breath of spring: *"Birth and death, love and loss, revolve around and around endlessly together."* I did not understand it, but I knew it and resented it.

But now all that was changed. My wise foreboding childhood had gone blind in a blaze of love and youth and passion. I was emerging from my first winter of unrequited longing and now the Mountain, the bursting spring, and my hope for love acknowledged and fulfilled, became merged into a single yearning song that I sung every waking moment and in my dreams. And when I thought of telling Avalee of my love for her, the imagined scene always and automatically unfolded in that cave under the cliff, and I heard my own half-whispered words softly reverberating within curving walls of stone.

"So this is your...your little secret cave?" She asked this question over her shoulder as she shuffled in on her hands and knees. Her long auburn hair, hanging down as she dipped her head to enter softly, erased the tiny tracks of field mice etched the night before in the powdered dust of the cave's floor. Her words were carried on a playful laugh. I stood outside, gulping and watching a patch of spring bluebirds swirl with a whispered chatter through the Blue Oaks above the cave. I could see her knees just showing in the lighted area of the enclosure. Her face was in shadow. I felt profoundly frightened at having brought her there, at what I was gathering courage to tell her there. I was sure that she was laughing at me.

"Well mountain boy, aren't you coming in to show me your cave? You said you wanted to show it to me."

"It isn't my cave really...exactly," I said in a flat voice. I was crawling into the shadows with her now. I felt the warmth of the inner stone on my back as I assumed my place next to her. I felt the warmth of her shoulder. "Actually someone else stayed in here a long time ago. There are some really old cooking things I found over in the corner under the rocks. There were some deer antlers bleached white hidden in here. There have been certain people coming here for a long time...I think for thousands of years. It's not mine really. I sort of belong to the cave, not the other way around." Talking like this, rattling away like this among these images and ideas, so deeply familiar, put me more at ease, pulled me back to deepness and oldness and solidity from that strange, terrifying youth and fragility and softness and sharpness of her. But as I finished speaking I turned my head in the shadows, eyes still dimmed from the brightness outside, and I saw that her face was not directed toward the light outside as I had thought it to be as I had spoken. Her face was turned directly to mine and her eyes were fixed on me, had been fixed on me all the while.

"So...when did you start coming up here alone?" She asked this softly and she was still looking directly at me. I felt paralyzed by her closeness. *If only I could just touch her*, I thought, *if only I could touch her hair or her face*. "For how long before you met me have you been coming here?" I felt a touch of something like resentment in her voice; something like...jealousy? Suspicion?

Without thinking of consequences I said, "I started coming here in dreams before I ever climbed up here. When I was about twelve I would wake up in a dream and I would climb through the attic onto the roof of my house and fly over the valley in a sort of dark-brown moonlight and float and fly over these peaks and rocks and I remember passing by this cave. Once I saw old books stacked in ancient shelves along the back wall..." I faltered, having no idea how either to conclude this confession or to continue it. "So I guess I have been coming up here since I was a little kid."

She paused and dropped her eyes for an instant, then looking up at me again she said, "I think you are making all of that up little cave boy." And as she said it I believed she was right and felt a cascading sensation within me, a dropping away of something precious but insubstantial, a sudden fading of a tenuous light that had sustained me. A wave of deep sadness swept over me. But at that very instant, at that very instant and but a moment more, she, without remark or warning, reached her hand to my face and gently, so gently, with a touch of such unbearable softness, placed her hand just below my eye and drew it slowly down my cheek as if she were tracing the course of a tear. All my senses stopped, all my breath suspended. A great breath caught me up and I was aware that I was gasping, gasping at what might come.

But her hand was gone, and in fact she had turned away slightly toward the light outside the cave. She did not speak now. She seemed to lean forward, peering down the slope below, peering through the poppies and the baby-blue-eyes, watching the bluebirds, tracing nonsense in the sand near her feet. I pressed myself back against the tender stone, holding myself firm there against it, knowing that it neither came forward toward me nor did it ever withdraw. I began to regain my balance.

Suddenly I realized she was humming a tune, softly, singing the strain of a familiar hymn, apparently absent-minded since she seemed absorbed with the spring day outside the cave.

"I come to the garden alone…" she sang softly, *"while the dew is still on the roses…and the voice I hear…falling on my ear…the Son of God discloses…"* this was an old hymn we both knew from childhoods in church.

She was singing whimsically, with a smile, with a playfulness that seemed gentle and lovely. *"And he walks with me, and he talks with me…and he tells me I am his own…. and the joy we share…as we tarry there…none other…has ever…known.* Don't you ever get lonely coming up here?" she suddenly asked as the tune ended, looking again directly at me. Then after a pause, "Or do you just pray mountain prayers and make up stories?"

For just an instant from the corner of my eye, I saw that she was gazing at me fixedly. I dropped my eyes, then bent my head involuntarily. My breathing was stifled. This question she had asked me was the perfect invitation for the confession I had longed to make to her those many wailing winter months. Now I felt my breath go flat and my heart die within me. I leaned slowly forward, placing my hands in the sand as if I were about to crawl desperately out of the cave. I was shaking nervously. I began to move forward.

As we had lingered within, huge April clouds had piled up over the Middle Mountain and now one lumbered across the sun. A sudden, deep shadow, nearly as dark as the cave's interior, fell over the entire world outside. In the instant of that shadow, as if cued by the secrecy of the cloud, she reached firmly for me, grasped my face in her hands, and bending to me with closed eyes, kissed me, warmly, warmly, her lips pressing deeply, long, then longer, she kissed me and released me. The cloud outside, revolving on currents unrelated to those on which we floated inside the cave, uncovered the world and all was instantly again bright grass and dancing flowers and singing birds and her warm breath in my ear.

IV

There was a day at the very end of a long ago springtime, a day in May when Avalee and I were playing like children on the hillsides of the Buttes in the tall grass. During the passing of the seasons this extravagant and playful girl and this brooding boy had wandered together through the mists of waterfalls, dangerously and thoughtlessly scaled the cliffs to our campfires in warm caves, and drifted through the poppies and lupines of Peace Valley. We had, in other words, circled and criss-crossed the enchanted island, holding hands ever more firmly, embracing ever more tightly in every mossy bower we discovered together, becoming ever more absorbed and enthralled by what was happening between us in this isolated and encompassing cluster of volcanoes.

Of course it is the usual thing for youngsters of this tender age to fall in love. It is just as usual for passion and certainty to waver and dissolve in the unconsidered hurricane of youth. But this youthful love did not waver. For me, the Mountain was a boundless permanence, an unqualified reality, an absolute

Presence in my life that from the very first transcended every other feature of the world. And since this girl, this auburn fairy, had become manifest in a youthful soul absorbed in the Mountain, she was for me a feature, a quality of the fundamental totality of that place. She had occurred for me utterly in the Mountain. She had come to me out of The Place.

And although I was aware of the subtle apprehension she felt at what must have seemed to her my "unnatural" and even somewhat pagan obsession with this feature of the earth, I was aware also that she knew that of all things, the Buttes and she who had come to me from them, were the most permanent, beloved and everlasting features in my world. The force of this knowledge between us was more compelling than all of the hesitance and uncertainty of youth. And although this would be far beyond the comprehension of any other human being in our lives, the two of us, tender, incredibly naïve and hardly more than children, were seduced by this enchanted mountain and its aura of fantasy and dream, into an utterly unlikely image of permanence, marriage and even babies. It was an image that it never occurred to us to doubt or even question.

So while this innocent seduction led us from many points on the Buttes' circumference, across countless undulating diameters, through every canyon and to every pinnacle, upon setting out to enter we were most often drawn back to the outer folds of Brockman Canyon. Here the Mountain had first invited us in. Here the viscous force of rising magma had folded valley sediments into the Buttes' most gentle hillsides; huge mounds as smooth and sensuous as the curves of youthful bodies.

We would hold each other tightly and roll down the soft hills, laughing in each other's ear. Coming to rest at the bottom with fading flowers all around, we would awkwardly kiss and lie still, sighing deeply. Lying there with her, I felt as if my whole body were filled with warm honey. I had no inclination to move at all, but she would begin to wiggle in a moment or two, struggle free from my embrace and go bounding through the wild oats with outstretched hands. I knew where she was going and followed slowly, across the dry creek bed, under the stooping live oaks toward the ruins of the old Brockman place, until I found her leaning against the only part of the prostrate ranch house still upright; a dark and peeling door that hung from one end of wall that curved downward like a twisted ribbon.

She was in the shadow of the leaning door, looking down, and her auburn hair had fallen across her eyes like a mask. Whenever we wandered in the Buttes, she every few minutes swept both slender hands through her hair to untangle it, then shook it out again and restored its normal mass of unruly curls. Her waist, very long and slender, curved almost unnaturally when she leaned against anything—a rock, an oak, an ancient, shingled wall. She almost always wore jeans, unintentionally ragged and tight. Her cowgirl style shirts were discolored a little with the stains of grass, but there was always a lovely, tattered, lacy frill drooping a little between the sweet hollow of her throat and the slight swelling of her breast. After such a day she had the faint scent of grass, moss, and clean, rich soil. Whenever we ran together in the Buttes, her eyes would take on a kind of doe-like, startled look and her full lips and flared nostrils made her completely irresistible and sometimes seem even a little dangerous. Now, rather hiding there in the shadow of that peeling, fallen door, she looked up very suddenly, startling me a little, her eyes wide and very bright and laughing. "OK, Caveman," she said forcefully. She had taken to calling me this now, rather than Caveboy. "My big strong caveman husband, I want you to carry me across the threshold of our lovely new home." Saying this, she gestured toward the pile of rubble behind her.

Avalee could not have weighed more than a hundred-ten pounds, even with the heavy, scuffed, half-collapsed riding boots she always insisted on hiking in. Whatever she wore, whatever her posture or her mood, she seemed to me overwhelmingly curvaceous, graceful and perfect, and if I noticed anything more than this, it was just how hopelessly scrawny I was in comparison, how totally unlikely a candidate for her interest I was. As a boy of 17 I probably didn't weigh in at very much more than she. Nevertheless the "Caveman" was going to do as his "bride" had commanded. I squared my shoulders and with a powerful flourish, scooped her up, kicked open the creaking door and stepped forward. Just beyond, the broken ruins of the old Brockman house lay in a dangerous-looking pile. But at my feet, a patch of deep greenery looked better and very inviting indeed. Avalee was laughing hysterically at my staggering pace and said desperately, "OK, OK, put me down! Put me down!" Here I smiled assuredly and tried to turn her a little to plant a tender kiss on her lips, but I lost my balance, stumbled and dropped her abruptly into the greenery. It was a patch of nettles.

Avalee was very fond of teasing, but she was compassionate of my humiliation, and besides, she loved me. But because of the nettles, I never forgot this first time we impersonated a couple in the ruins of that pioneer house together in the Buttes, never forgot how completely I had failed to bear her up, and how nevertheless complete was the trust and confidence she had granted me by this teasing reference to me as her "big, strong husband". It was an entirely mutual trust and by these girlish comments and gestures, she had completely swept away all of my scrawny doubts and filled me with a foolish *amour-propre*. So it was only natural that I should escort my lady up the andesite castles and help her over the rocks to the cave. It was a familiar place for us by now, and the fire-ring had been warmed only a few evenings before. I would become increasingly worshipful in a jubilant kind of way as we climbed, and she would become a little subdued and somber by the time we arrived, as if she felt a vague disapproval at the heathenish sort of wildness that always overtook me as we ascended. We scooted in and leaned, wrapped around each other, against the cave wall. By now the sun was low in Bragg's Canyon and a beam of red light fell directly on her face. With my lips near her ear, I could see the soft down on her cheek, gossamer and luminous in the light. I could see the curve of her neck, unbearably soft and gentle. I could smell her hair and just a touch of her favorite perfume—I think she had said it was called White Shoulders. "Now this is our *real* home," I whispered in her ear. "This is where we have lived for a thousand years...and this is where we should live for a thousand years more."

She squirmed away again, but now stretched out in the sand, her fawn-head resting in my lap. I helplessly began sifting through her long auburn curls. She was silent for quite a long time, breathing deeply and thinking. "Well," she said, "that's all fine and good, that's another very nice story." She very slowly turned her head, still firmly in my lap, like a caress, until she was looking up into my eyes. "But you know, you silly boy, that in a thousand years we will be in heaven with Jesus. That is if you don't tell too many lies...and believe them too much". Her voice became very soft, very tentative. "But anyway, don't you think that when we grow up we should move into an actual, wooden house?" Now suddenly she was on her knees before me, her warm arms around my neck, speaking in a sort of baby talk while she kissed me with little kisses. "You know...the babies.... can't...be born... in a cave...like you probably were."

Daylight is slowly failing and it has become dark and shadowy in the cave. Avalee wants to absorb the last of the day's brightness, and now we are sitting in the drying grass outside, wanting to be a little warmer in the waning day, wanting to show ourselves to the blue sky and the blue birds. We are tired and happy and we have only a few minutes before we must wind our way, hand in hand, down from the mountain, past the silent grotto where in the late, drying spring, the waterfall has become only a ghostly memory, down the patched road to the east and back through the orchards beneath the big trees to the warm, white house. The sun sinks, sinks, until it touches the point of rock that towers over that trickster crevice a hundred yards beyond, turns into a giant six-pointed star of light for just a moment, then flicks out of sight leaving behind a turquoise sky. "The night is the best," I tell her assuredly. "The owls start swirling around…like ghosts. The spirits come out and start teaching us things."

She jabs me in the ribs. "The *Holy Spirit* teaches us things when we study the Bible," she says. "Preferably in church or at least in a warm house."

Now she leans to me, pressing her head into my neck. "It's getting cold," she says. Then after a pause, "And it's getting lonely up here."

I feel nothing of this loneliness except a quiet desperation at what she has said. I always long for the coming of darkness in these wild places deep in the Buttes and feel reluctant to depart as a day ends. The evening and the setting sun have called up the mountain wind, and there is a moaning and a sighing in the air, and the tall amber-green grass is undulating like water. Like an expansive, invisible animal, the wind rolls around us for a moment, then presses the grass and stirs the oak leaves as it flows over the brink and into Bragg's Canyon. There is a scent like roasting grain on the breeze, the grass drying in the warming season. My eyes have followed the moving air into the canyon, and there just below me floats a tattered banner of spider silk, lighter than the air, backlit by the sinking sun, fixed and connected to nothing in the universe, utterly surrendered to ambiguity. For a moment, this little drifting ghost leads my eye to the old cabin where a few years before I had been lost in the wet night. Avalee's distant mood there in that high place makes me think for a moment that she, like the wind-lost web, might be floated away far from me on the evening currents, and I want to hold her, anchor her to my life and to this mountain island, life and mountain now the same, no longer distinguishable one from the other. Now I am desperate to tack her down; now I am the landscape itself, wanting to haunt and possess her here forever, where we belong together.

"Look," I say, "look down there, Av. Down in the bottom of the canyon. See that little brown cabin down there?"

She looks now down into the deepening shadows of Bragg's canyon where that old cabin has almost disappeared into the evening. "Yes," she murmurs uneasily, "Yes, I can see it just barely."

"Can you see the little candles twinkling in the windows through the curtains? Can you see the smoke coming from the chimney? Can you see us rocking out on the porch in the twilight? Can you hear the owls on the roof telling us they love us?"

Avalee is disconcerted a little by this, as she always is with my dreams. And I am just a little apprehensive, as I always am when I tell them to her. But she doesn't tease. She doesn't smile. She speaks in a very small voice and I am frightened a little at the touch of sadness, at the moistness of her eyes. "Yes," she whispers. " Yes, I can see us down there."

This canyon of the cabin is a deep elongate bowl lying very near the center of the volcanic aureole, like the ovary of a flower. Two opposite sides of the bowl sweep upward a thousand feet like hands cupped at the wrists, fingers open. The dark eyes of caves squint from sheer cliff-faces lined with chaparral brows. One of them is the warm chamber of our passion. One end of the canyon is enclosed by a peak shaped like a heart, the other, where an old wagon road enters from the west, by another waterfall cascading in winter and spring down a switch-back ladder of sculpted rock covered with espaliered and clinging shrubs. Over the undulating canyon bottom of perhaps a hundred acres spreads the most ancient and venerable forest of Blue Oaks in the Buttes, trees the arms of a boy would not reach around, huge leafy globes luminous about twisted limb, branch and twig. These green to russet canopies shade a sweep of the richest grasses, thickest and tallest beneath the trees, in springtime sprinkled with lupine and poppy everywhere. Through this hidden garden, east to west, sings the Buttes' largest stream. Over the stream tower huge Valley Oaks, cottonwood and a few sycamores, dwarfing the Blues further out. The seasonal waters swirl and bubble over a mosaic of smoothed volcanic cobbles, turning past boulders on both sides. Along the thickest part of the riparian corridor, deep mortars where ancient hands have rhythmically pounded the fruit of the oaks are sprinkled every twenty feet on the flattest boulders. In the Buttes' round island of wild, rocky beauty this canyon, as it is in 1964 is the richest jewel.

Right at its center, a few yards off the streamside, stood this little brown cabin, no larger than a bungalow's bedroom. Its plank floor was supported by a thin foundation of cream-colored rhyolite slabs. The shakes of its walls were still intact, although splintered, eroded and almost black with age. It was the simplest of structures, just a box with a peaked roof, two small empty windows and a door quite in the center, which opened toward my little cave high above. Yet someone a hundred years before had adorned bare necessity with a sense of grace. At the door was a small patio of sorts, paved with flagstones of white, gray and deep brown. Someone had searched up and down the stream for pleasing shapes, water-smoothed on top, and had carefully fitted them together. There was a tidy border of old brick defining the porch, and pineapple weed that looked like wild chamomile was growing in the pattern of cracks between the flagstones. The door was made of three rutted, hand-hewn planks, but the handle, broken and hanging from an angular hand-made nail, was a manzanita fork, curved and smooth.

I was standing beneath a tree watching Avalee step slowly toward the cabin. Now she reached for the door, having to lean forward as if hesitant to stand too close. She poked her head into the shadow, peering inside. A rag of dirty fabric flapped a little from the window. She withdrew her head, looked back at me with a crooked smile and stepped inside. Instantly, but with complete silence, an owl, snowy white from beneath, swooped from the apex of the roof and wheeled away into the creek-side trees.

"Woops, there goes your owl," she said. " I guess he doesn't love us *that* much."

I followed her inside. It was a dark, fragrant enclosure, sliced by thin lines of very bright sunlight that beamed in through many holes in the roof. A hundred winters had almost dissolved the shingles. Inside, the air seemed baked, smelling of dust, dry wood, bird nests and ash.

I found a broken shake outside and began to scoop the caked ash from the stove, then with some baling wire, re-attached the cast-iron door and rusty, fragile stovepipe. She found the stub of an old broom behind the wood-stove and swept the place down, then gave it a final dusting with handfuls of dried moss. Some yellow wallflowers were all that remained of the spring bloom out in the weeds, but we gathered as many as we could find and pressed them into the broken neck of a bluish bottle from out back. Others we stuck in the cracks around the window. While she sat in the shade by the creek behind the cabin, I ran up the slope and brought back armloads of bay laurel boughs. While she watched, I spread these thickly over the rusty spring of the small metal cot. When we lay down in each other's arms, the scent of the bay rose up around us like a concealing cloud. That bouquet of bay, always compelling, always reaching deep into me and somehow pungently pinching some inaccessible feature of my senses, now surrounded us like liquid, and amidst soft kisses, brushings of lips, fevered caresses and murmurings, it really felt that we were as hidden as if we had been floating in a deep, still pool.

All though these first five years of my Middle Mountain wandering, I had been always alone, until Avalee. I had become familiar with batches of wary young steers, dimly trusting and slow-moving sheep, curiously unalarmed deer, many skittering and shy smaller creatures like ringtails, raccoons and porcupines, but never had I encountered, even seen from a distance, another human being. Every now and then I had heard a very distant snarl of a chainsaw, even once or twice a shout, like someone driving livestock far out of sight. Now suddenly, as we became more and more absorbed in the touch and taste of each other, floating in that liquid pool of laurel-scent, I realized with a shock, the deep rumbling of an engine right outside the cabin.

Both of us bobbed to the surface like corks, faces flushed, instantly ashamed, deeply alarmed and frightened. This was the first time such a sense of culpability had come to us, two teenagers discovered in a hidden place. I was confused and didn't know what to make of what was happening. All of the pieces of this did not fit coherently together. Somehow, since I had only ever arrived here through miles of broken wilderness, since entering I had passed into another dimension the reality of which fairly erased the world outside, it had never even occurred to me that a road could bring a vehicle into this deepness. I was shocked. Quickly we were on our feet, smoothing and buttoning our rumpled cloths, suppressing disheveled hair, painfully aware that we had to come outside or most likely be discovered by someone unknown bursting into the cabin, aware also that when we did our flushed faces and nervous manner would utterly give us away. Avalee seemed, really, about to cry. I had never seen her afraid before. I reached for her a little but she drew back. "What...what shall we do?" she pleaded.

Swallowing hard in order to speak, I said, "Just go on out. Just go out." And we creaked open the old door and stepped into the blinding light.

There, not twenty feet from the cabin against the backdrop of the terraced wall of Bragg's Canyon, was a big battered green flatbed truck. On the flatbed were strewn coils of rope, many twisted bunches of baling wire, lengths of gate, some buckets, many burlap sacks, some empty, some stuffed full. The truck rocked slowly with the idling engine. An old man stood in the open door, one leg raised to the running board, one arm draped over the window. He wore round spectacles on a rather round, sunburned face. He was a man of middle height but his rumpled overalls piled above immense work boots, and a khaki shirt that bulged out all around the overalls, made him look shorter. Thatches of gray hair stuck out a little around the edges of his ears from beneath a very dirty old felt hat, sweat and dirt-blackened near his forehead. Behind the smudged lenses, his eyes were serious and a little surprised. He did not smile.

Yet, after all of my shock, upon actually seeing him there looking at us, I did not feel any longer in the least apprehensive. There was nothing about him that seemed threatening at all. So I cleared my throat, tried on a grimace in an attempt to smile and look relaxed, and croaked, "Hello!"

With my skinny adolescent awkwardness, draped in those brown cords, green flannel, and tattered moccasins I always wore in the Buttes, I must have appeared really comical, affected, and most of all, agonized. Now his face crinkled into a slow smile. He first looked me very steadily up and down, then glanced at Avalee and smiled again, this time with unaffected pleasure. Almost instantly she had seen his twinkling eyes, and in her never long-repressed self-assurance, knowing somehow how remarkable and unexpected a sight she was, standing in front of that crumbling hutch near his rough, ungainly truck, she sang out a greeting in her pretty voice, with her pretty face. "Hi there!" she fluted, waving. "How are you doing?"

"Well... I'll be goddamned," he said in a really mellow and gentle voice. "I'll be goddamned," again, as if once was not enough. "This is a goddamned first!" Now his eyes left us and slowly moved over the cabin, to the drooping, open door, to the shadows inside concealing the old stove and the old cot, which he most certainly knew were there. The smile faded and was replaced with a look of mock severity, squinting eyes, and pursed lips. He slowly reached up and removed his spectacles. He even more slowly reached down and killed the engine. Now I could see that although he was without any malice or real annoyance, he most certainly was going to torture us a little.

"Now what in hell are you two youngsters doing way the hell up here?"

"Oh...well...we were just hiking around," I said, trying to gain confidence. "Uh, you know, enjoying the scenery...exploring."

"Yup," he said. "Yup...enjoying the scenery." Then his voice became much less serious and he really wasn't even trying to restrain his amusement. "And, say, how was the scenery there in the old cabin?"

Now, although my own face was burning again and what little self-assurance I had gathered about me had entirely evaporated, I could feel a sort of heat, a sort of belligerence emanating from the slender girl standing beside and a little behind me. I knew from experience that it would be a sweet, almost imploring kind of belligerence, but my apprehension increased measurably when she stepped forward a little with her hands on her hips and her head, tossing the auburn hair from her eyes, leaned jauntily to one side. I looked over at her. Her cheeks were very red. There was a snap in her eyes. She opened her mouth to speak, but he stepped forward rapidly to us, extended his hand and said, "Tony...name is Tony."

"Well, it's a pretty nice little old cabin," he continued very hurriedly. His voice sounded softer, a bit apologetic for the very mild ribaldry of his "scenery" comment. "And I hope you youngsters like it...and are having a great time hiking around. Wonderful place up here! Best place I have ever been.... hey! Here they come! Here come the boys with the sheep!"

He turned from us now and amidst a yammering and bleating, the barking of dogs, dust, and the clanging of bells, a bunch of about two-hundred sheep burst from the thick woodland a hundred yards from us to the east. Behind them came two young fellows carrying long staffs with metal hooks on the ends, and several darting, slinking, mottled and piebald dogs nipped treacherously at ovine heels. Some of these creatures looked worn and droopy, old mothers of many lambs. Others, the same size or even larger, were robust and if possible for a sheep, even muscular. All of them were embarrassingly undressed, their bodies crossed and striped with the rapid passings of the sheers. However silly they looked, they no doubt felt pretty good without the wool, for there was a mood of excitement in the crowd.

They drew closer and the man at the truck turned to us again and said, "Gathering. Gathering up this last bunch. Water all gone except for that puddle up the trail, and this bunch had gotten way over onto Bradys'. We couldn't find the sons-a-bitches till today."

We were all interested now and the uncomfortable scene at the cabin door was completely forgotten. By now the whole disheveled flock was crowding around the truck, probably expectant of corn or alfalfa or some other handout. The dogs plopped like rags immediately in the shade. The two young herders stood behind, gawking unabashedly at Avalee and me, primarily at Avalee, no doubt most unexpected and strange to them. They were both very stocky young guys, ruddy of complexion, almost red, with black shocks of upright hair, so thick there was clearly too much of it for their heads. The old man seemed aware what an object of odd fascination we must be to his herders. He shouted a few words to them in a language that I knew was not Spanish but did not recognize further. Instantly the dogs leapt up, and like extensions of the herders, skillfully pushed the sheep away from the truck under some large oaks where there still was a touch of green to the tall grass.

Now we are all three, Avalee, the old man and I, sitting together on the flagstones, leaning against the cabin. "Yep," he was saying, "we got the rest—almost two-thousand—out three weeks ago. Nothing here now for them anymore."

"But the grass is still green under the trees," suggested Avalee.

He smiled at her whenever she spoke. "A little green, sure, but nothing in it for sheep-feed anymore. All headed out besides. Foxtails, stickery seeds, ripgut…nothing for them. And hardly any water. We always push them out about now."

"Where too?" I asked.

"Well, all the way out of the Buttes, out to West Butte Road, across Butte Sink and into the bean fields, mostly," he said with real interest. "From there the market trucks come for the yearlings and the ewes munch around out there with the bucks. Just twenty or thirty bucks for a couple-thousand ewes. Those bastards screw themselves to death. They die young." Then suddenly, in the midst of this habitual and natural talk, he realized Avalee was sitting there. He wasn't embarrassed and neither was she, but he did say, "Sorry." She laughed and said that she was a country girl and that it was OK. " They stay there with the herders until next winter's rains," he continued. "Then back up into the Bragg place. Like that every year." There was a pause. "For many, many years."

I was fascinated by these alert, powerful and incredibly shy workers. "Where are the herders from?" I asked.

"Jess and Manuel? They're Basque, from Spain, from the Pyrenees. They speak Basque, not Spanish. They contract over here for four or five years. I pay 'em four or five-hundred a month along with their food and wine and they follow the sheep. Five years working here and a lot of them can go home and buy their own ranches. Good boys. The best." I remembered now, climbing around in various caves and rock shelters, especially above Peace Valley, seeing strange inscriptions etched in charcoal on the walls of the caves. I remembered one name, "Estachio Zunda", that had seemed exotic and beautiful to me, scrawled above an indecipherable date. I had been mystified at the time with the language of the graffiti, which had a bizarre, mysterious look squiggled on the rocks.

"Where do they live while they're watching the sheep?" Avalee asked. The old man smiled again very beamingly.

"Sheep wagons, cook houses," he said. "Little cabins on wheels with curved roofs and with a stove and cots inside…like in the cabin here." He paused and cleared his throat. "Drag 'em around with a pickup or tractor wherever we move the sheep. Damn hassle getting a wagon up here though. The road into this canyon is almost too rough, but the grass is the best in the Buttes. We barely got the wagon out this year. That's why that cabin was built. A long time ago."

Now there was a long period of silence. We could no longer see Jess and Manuel and the sheep were almost invisible under the wide Blue Oak canopy. The dogs were gone somewhere. I could vaguely hear shouts and barks and thought of the herders and dogs rambling up in the rocks. "What do they have to watch the sheep for?" I asked. "Can't you just let them graze around up here?"

"Ha!" The man's laugh came like a derisive blast. "Goddamn coyotes kill 'em! Goddamn bobcats eat 'em! If those boys weren't always up here patrolling around with guns, shooting those goddamn bastards, why I'd loose half my herd." This sounded like an exaggeration to me, but still, the image of the vigilant herders protecting innocent lambs was appealing. Now he was silent again, seeming to be deep in thought. A Redtail screeched high above and from the trees came the hollow sound of a sheep bell with a smothered clank in a slow cadence. A very warm breeze stirred the oak leaves all around and barely moved the cabin door in a low squeak. He looked suddenly up at me, and the twinkle had returned to his eyes. "You spend a lot of time up here, young man?" he asked.

Without thinking I said, "Oh yes…since I was a kid. I've been all over the Buttes." Now I paused a long time. "This is the most beautiful… the most special, magical place in the world." Immediately I felt embarrassed as always happened when these uncontrollable utterances poured out of me, and I felt Avalee looking at me a little sharply.

"Yep…yep. I know what you mean. I have a boy, older than you, already in business back east, and I'll be damned if he didn't manage to buy a little chunk of land up on the top of Goat Rocks. I think he wants to build a castle. But you now…since you're so crazy about these Buttes, how 'bout this idea? Isn't exactly a castle, but I provide all the shakes and shingles, all the lumber, all the nails. You do the work and make this old cabin watertight and livable, and I set you up here next season with a bunch of sheep and put you to work. Pay you the same as these boys, except for the vino and smokes," he chuckled. "Then I won't have to try and drag that damned wagon up here! How about that?"

I can't even begin to express what a sense of unbridled, childish joy swept over me as he said these words. Here someone was matter-of-factly offering to manifest for me a beautiful dream in the waking world. The image of this cabin, primly restored, flowers growing around the rhyolite porch, a rocking chair out front, the stove glowing warmly inside, the windows hung with clean white curtains undulating slowly in a spring breeze, a quiet group of somehow well-scrubbed, white sheep grazing contentedly all around the house, and I—I in the rocking-chair, rocking slowly like a potentate in bliss, in the midst of it all—this image appeared...no, it flashed behind my eyes with an instantaneous, crystalline clarity that made me dizzy for a moment. And central to the image was Avalee; Avalee nestled on my lap on the old rocking-chair, snuggling her lips into my neck while we watched some pleasantly amorphous babies crawling before us in the flowers.

I was breathing heavily. "Oh, sure! Oh sure!" I gushed. "That would be the greatest thing in the world...."

Avalee abruptly interrupted me. She spoke in a soft but insistent, undeniable voice. "But what about school?" she said. " What about your parents?"

Now this many-corded, harmonic symphony of image that had gushed through me at Tony's words was muffled to a drone, a deep, heavy note that pressed down on me and seemed to plug my ears. I realized instantly that Tony, seeing me with this girl two years older than myself, with my somewhat overly mature manner, had really no way whatsoever to have determined my exact age and position in life. The whole scene was swept away as he suddenly laughed. "Why, this young lady is absolutely right, of course. You're parents would never allow such a thing. I wouldn't have! She's absolutely right. What an idea! Hey Jess! Hey Manual! Let's get 'em up and out of here!" And even as he spoke, he was on his feet, walking rapidly away from us, not even looking back. His back was turned and he was elsewhere absorbed, so Avalee leaned quickly toward me and kissed me softly and moistly on the cheek. Then she jumped to her feet and ran without hesitation toward the sheep and seemed to merge with them as they swarmed up and around the truck amidst the shouts and yapping dogs. I still sat, alone, against the old cabin, tears rising to my eyes, my throat aching, feeling the slivers from the broken shakes beginning to stick into the skin of my back.

I leaned against the cabin wall for what seemed a very long time, watching the sheep cluster together into a dusty bunch, harassed by nipping dogs and shouting herders. The battered green truck had moved on ahead and I could only hear it very faintly. I was watching intently for Avalee, puzzled a little at how long she had been gone, but I knew it would be typical of her to enjoy running after an energetically shuffling herd of sheep. I knew also that at such moments it would be unlikely she would be thinking about me and my over-tender sensibilities. But when she emerged from the cloud of dust and approached me, it was apparent from her solemn, unsmiling face and the worried crinkles on her brow, that seeing me sitting there still, unmoving and morbid while she had scampered away with the sheep, had disturbed her.

Without hesitating she said, as she approached me, "Come on Cave Man. Let's climb."

Blue and Interior Live Oaks, some huge and robust, some twisted and dwarfed, stand in regiments over almost every hillside in the Middle Mountain. Much larger, big-leafed Valley, or White Oaks, not so numerous, occupy nearly all of the deeper soils. Accompanying the oaks, a few ancient sycamore and many more cottonwoods forest the creek-sides. Manzanita, some very old and very large, outshine with their smooth, amber skins, the Toyon, Scrub Oak and Buckbrush that clog the chaparral thickets. One lone Ponderosa, the only pine tree in the Buttes, grows near the summit of one of the highest peaks, its origins a mystery. But sprinkled, mostly at lower elevations on the dryer, more barren southern fringe of the Middle Mountain, are occasional California Juniper, a hardy, drought-resistant, shrubby conifer with stringy bark and very short, serrated fans of oily cedar-like needles, pungent and aromatic. Few and relatively young, growing generally only on this southern fringe of the volcanic circle, these junipers always seemed to me like visitors, a little exotic in the Buttes.

But far away, across the wild, undulated rosette of the Buttes, miles to the north of these younger stands of juniper and completely solitary in the whole of the northern two-thirds of the volcanic cluster, is, for me, the most remarkable tree in the Buttes. Growing right out of a root-widened crack in a rough andesite spire, hidden high and clingingly in an alcove about the size of an eagle's nest on the cliff face a hundred yards from our cave, is the twisted, tortured old juniper that I had found while wandering lost in the darkness, over four years before I first guided Avalee to the cave. I had visited this tree many times during that four years, and although at the time I knew and thought little about the relative ages of trees, I had, with my parents, visited the California Redwoods, and I recognized in this cliff-hanging juniper something of great age. It is very likely one of the oldest living things in the Middle Mountain.

This tree seemed filled with conscious power. From the first moment I saw her, I knew her as a beautiful, living being who was aware of my presence. She seemed naturally to reach for me, embracing me, and when I wrapped my arms about her and clung to her, there would pour from me cascades of feeling, sometimes causing me to weep. I cried with a sense of unbearable recognition and comfort. I spontaneously named her *Mother* when I pressed my face to her rough and twisted trunk and whispered to her. And I would hear her voice murmuring to me as *Child*.

She was *such* a deep, deep secret, that even when I finally led Avalee to her, I never spoke of these things. Although there was no doubt in me about this tree, I was aware that these feelings, perceptions and behavior could be thought of as quite abnormal and disturbing to other people in the world, so much so that Avalee, even Avalee, could not be told.

As we ascend, the sky has become overcast and gray, unusual for a day so late in spring. We are sitting beneath Mother Juniper, but there is a thickness to the air, made of subtle tension and a sense of sorrow, that keeps us apart. I am leaning against the ragged trunk of the tree. Avalee is crouched at the alcove's outer edge, leaning over the cliff, gazing into the chasm. I am watching her back and can see that her chin is resting on her hands, supported by the rocky lip of the alcove. There is a light breeze from the south and it is very slowly stirring her hair. We both know quite well what has suppressed us this way. It is that collision that occurred at the cabin, the collision between my thoughtless, absolute vulnerability to pretty dreams and mystic visions, and the firmness of her happy, tenacious, energetic grip on the real and the solid composition of the world. We are disturbed and a little confused also by the sense of our disagreement, colliding with the unqualified, doubtless, passionate dedication that we both know is eternal, inescapable and precious between us. I am morose and in a darkened spirit. Avalee is mildly annoyed and intolerant of this disruption of our usually unmitigated happiness together. She is confident that her persistent, irrefutable joy at the general state of things, can push through this heavy atmosphere that has fallen over us, and reunite us in our typical thoughtless harmony. Knowing her as I do, I am well aware of all of this, but I feel injured in a very tender part of myself and I am going to be stubborn, melodramatic, and difficult.

"Come on over here and sit with me," she says. Silently and frowning, I just press myself more firmly against the juniper. She turns rapidly around, rustling sharply in the grass and faces me. Pausing, she tightens her lips. Then her face softens and there is just a hint of a playful smile. "What are you so mad about?" she asks.

I answer very softly and evenly: "I am not mad at all."

"Oh yes you are. It's because of what I said about you being a sheep herder," she says. "It's because you don't like it whenever anybody tells you your dreams are just dreams and maybe you shouldn't take them so seriously."

"No," I answer, "not just anybody, just you, just when you tell me that, because I trust you more than anyone in the world and I tell you true secrets that I would never tell anyone else." She can see that there are tears in my eyes, but as always with her, compassion is mixed with firmness, and she smiles a little and scoots a bit closer to me, sitting in the grass, hugging her knees.

"I know, I know," she says, a little distress creeping into her voice. "I really do love your stories and your dreams most of the time, but you know, there is a difference between things we imagine and make up and things that are *really* true in the world." Then she adds very tenderly, very softly, "Like the difference between imagining how fun it would be to live up here in the Buttes in a sheep-herder's cabin, and knowing you have to go to school and go to church and obey your parents..." now she speaks playfully, "...and be a *good* boy."

"Yes," I say in a rather hard, flat voice. "Like the difference between the stories and fantasies you read in the Bible and hear in church, and the real, true things you can hear here, in this place. And if 'being a good boy' means believing that school and church are the only places to learn what is true, and always believing what my parents say is true…well, I don't think that is being good at all."

"You can't really mean that you think it is right to disrespect and disobey what your parents teach you," she says. "You can't really mean that." I am annoyed and argumentative still, but in spite of her familiar dogmatic resistance, the unmistakable, imploring sweetness of her tone begins to melt me, and to melt this thick barrier between us. She has moved a little toward me as she has spoken, and I am leaning now away from the tree, my head a little closer to hers. But I am still full of the arrogance of my worshipful certainty about my magic mountain and all that it fills me with, still wheedled by the power of a sharp but raw seventeen-year-old intellect, still so sure of my command of this Christian foolishness.

"No," I answer almost under my breath. "No, I don't mean that. But I do mean that it's very silly to think that what is real and makes sense is some 'Heaven' somewhere else in the universe and not to know that the world is perfect right here." Now almost sharply, "Perfect for me…and I thought perfect for us."

As I have spoken, I have turned away from Avalee and find myself facing the tree, my arms around the twisted trunk. I can smell the dry spice of the bark. The wind has stilled. Clutching the juniper a little savagely, I feel stirred with the force and power of my own words, with the clarity of my insight. I picture her quiet and thoughtful there behind me, considering my wisdom.

But Avalee, Avalee who has pierced into my little heart as forcefully and ruthlessly as has this wild weapon of a mountain, Avalee, whose humanness and firmness of spirit cannot be moved by my boyish polemics, starts to sing to me in her high, pure sweet girl's voice, and although she is behind me I can see the gentle, forgiving, understanding smile on her face. *"This world is not my home...I'm just a-passing through...my treasures are laid up...somewhere beyond the blue...the angels beckon me...from heaven's open door...and I can't...feel at home...in this world...anymore."*

But right in the swell of boundless love her voice produces in me, there is also a stirring of humiliation and impotence, and an argument twists like a worm in my stomach and begins to rise. I take a breath to speak but in some clear confusion of senses I hear the voice of the tree sharply and she says to me, *Hush! Leave her alone! You're insistence is cruel and foolish!* At that instant, Avalee has rushed to me, pressing her breast to my back and her open thighs tight about my legs and her face to my neck and her warmth and her scent wrap around me and I feel that her face is wet and hot with crying, when I thought she had been laughing at me. Flooded with remorse, I turn to her and she is clinging to my neck and enclosing me. We are pressing and crushing the Mother Juniper's bark and leaf and her earthen acid scent curls and swirls and surrounds our fevered movements.

Look down there far below; there is this small, round, rocky kingdom, floating near the flat wet earth in the gray sky; there is this shard of rock rising from a broken volcano; there is this ancient, twisted mother tree clutching the rock, almost too far below to be seen. And far, far too tiny to be seen at all, are these two foolish, blessed, endangered children, gasping and loving down there in the very heart of the world.

V

In the warm dark of a summer night not long after, I crept from my bed where I had been restlessly tossing in a maelstrom of thoughts and dreams and drifted through the open window of my room. I padded softly down the walk and into the orchards. The exhalations of ripening peaches and dark, stewing soil seep into my pores, and the faint scent of pesticides, mistaken in boyhood ignorance for a natural part of this bouquet of homeland, sting just a little in my eyes. Then, in an hour, there is the gracious sweetness of dry grass on the rising rampart hills of the Middle Mountain, a fresh breath from the mouth of a distant canyon, a little cooler than the heated valley night all around. On and on down the broken twisted road, over the last rise to the open arms of Brockman Canyon, always reaching for me, waiting to take me in and hush me to sleep from the fervor that had driven me from my bed.

But the way is guarded. I see, standing at the canyon's mouth the sword of the cherubim gripped in upraised arm, flaming terribly in the Buttes' blackness. At least this is the first vague image that comes to me as I discover that out on the flat at canyon's mouth where the angular skeleton of a drilling rig had a few weeks before been boring into the unguessed anatomy of the mountain's apron, now a productive gas well was being flared, an immense, whipping flame roaring from the mouth of a hole that had been bored three-thousand feet into the earth. It burns like something I have never imagined in the Mountain, a huge elevated torch in the black empty night. Steeped in the Genesis fable from the cradle, I think of the Tree of Life and its Fruit of Forbidden Knowledge, of the Serpent Cursed, of the Shame of Nakedness, of Exile From the Garden, of Eden's gate guarded by an angel with a burning sword, and all of those murky and unsettling images of the Temptress Mother of Fallen Man. This ancient stuff swirls in me for just an instant like a dust-devil gathering up a few images of Avalee and the Mother Juniper into its vortex, and then is washed away by the purity and certainty of the Mountain's higher holiness, miraculously mine even in childhood without doubt or allegory.

No, the way is not barred. I am no longer a party to that Covenant. I am not among those cast from the garden in foolish shame. I had been blown well past all of that even as a boy by the Mountain's pagan wind. This vaporous hydrocarbon cherubim whose righteous sword burns with a fire fueled from the Pit frightens me not at all. It is easy to slip on past. Tonight I have a very special reason to be lifted by the Mountain into the night sky. Tonight I am especially directed to kneel atop my andesite spire, gaze back down to the lights of my hometown, even to the lights of my father's house. For tonight I have decided I must ponder deeply telling him something I have only just learned: that I must leave his house forever.

I wonder at myself now, when I remember how at seventeen I led my father up the stairway for a talk in my room, with a mind clear of anxiety, pure and focused of purpose, without a breath of hesitation about the future. Once, a couple of years before, he had watched me come in the back door with my muddy moccasins and oak-leaves in my hair from thirty hours exulting alone in the Buttes. He had come to my room, placed me squarely in front of him and told me, "I am concerned. A normal, healthy, well-adjusted boy just does not climb out of windows in the middle of the night and go running around up in the hills by himself without telling anybody. I think we might need to get some professional help for you." He was accustomed to being sometimes amused, sometimes alarmed, sometimes deeply puzzled at some of the pronouncements I made to him when we talked of things religious and serious. I was a very difficult son, not intentionally rebellious, but unsettlingly precocious, just completely inscrutable, filled with all sorts of unexpected grandiloquence and creative extravagance. But in spite of this, perhaps because of this, my proud and loving parents foresaw my future unfurling in a productive, accomplished pattern. They of course saw these juvenile rivulets of passion flowing into one of the life-courses familiar and admirable to them.

Now this night I have issued from the Mountain that has seized my soul and brought me my first love, filled with faith in the immutability and rectitude of that love, utterly and doubtlessly authorized by that orogenic Source to turn so very early in life from the broad avenue of childhood into a soaring, twisted and ecstatic path. And while innocent of cruelty, I will do this cruelly into my father's unexpecting face. And amazingly there is no hesitation or uncertainty in me at all.

He has been sitting near the fireplace, sitting in the burnished darkness of the dying coals, waiting I am sure, for me. Although his face is in shadow, I see a reprimand there and his lips part to deliver it, but I say rapidly, "Dad, I want to talk to you…upstairs." He says OK, go on ahead, and we begin climbing those hundred-year-old stairs, impossibly narrow and steep, twenty-two difficult steps, up and down which my mother has trudged with my clothes to wash, fresh fragrant bedding for us, up and down for the years of my childhood here. The hallway upstairs is dark, my siblings long asleep in their rooms, my exhausted mother breathing deeply in her bed. The full, summer-leafed oaks are brushing my room's many windows in the warm breeze outside. The only other sound is the garrulous improvisation of a Northern Mockingbird who almost always comes this time of night to sit and sing atop the arched lightpost out front. My father sits down at my desk and picks up one of my school textbooks, thumbing through it, glancing now at the pages, now up to me where I am standing before him. He might be thinking of some of the perplexing ideas I have submitted to him in the past. He might be thinking that I am going to lodge some complaint or offer some suggestion about my 'oppressive and irrelevant' schoolwork. He may even expect some tortured discussion of my adolescent romance, of which he is certainly aware. But he has no expectation whatsoever when I say without preface or preamble, "Dad….Avalee is going to have a baby."

Outside I hear the harsh wail of the owl and the mockingbird falls suddenly silent. There is a catch in my father's breath and a rapid, rasping exhalation. What cherished, long and carefully nurtured parental dreams for my life he sees extinguished behind his dark eyes, what agony flashes through him in that instant of my disclosure, I cannot know. The silence seems long. The room is filled with my father's feeling: dense, powerful, sorrowful and bitter. But it is anger I hear when he says huskily, "How long has this been going on! Where! Up there in those *buttes*?"

I am still standing over him and his head now is deeply bowed to his chest. Never when I had been so swiftly abducted on that first morning atop the tower, never when I began those childish flying dreams, never when he had reclaimed me from that long, wandering black night of my initiation, never when I cried and prayed in deep canyons, never when I had tasted sacred passion in the high rocks, had I ever once breathed a word of any of this to him. Gentle, firm, imperious, devoted, religious father that he was, this numinous and errant life of mine is a realm he could never have entered. So I answer him simply and evenly, "Those questions make no difference now. All that is important now is my life with Avalee and the baby." And at this, without even a pause, he jerks suddenly to his feet and walks rapidly out of the room closing my door very heavily behind him.

Deep in the night I lay on my bed. I have opened all of my windows to let in the soothing night, but there is no sound outside, nothing stirring of owl or mockingbird or insect or even breeze in leaves. The scent of the Mountain's drying grass, pungent and distinct from the irrigated orchards, fills my head and overwhelms me. And dimly, muffled through the walls of the old house, I hear my mother sobbing and sobbing and sobbing in my father's arms until just before dawn, in the darkness of their room.

***

I was grateful my parents happened not to be at home when Avalee and her mother pulled into the driveway beneath the big oaks to pick me up. Only a few hours before, my father had pushed a note into my hand—his signature below words of parental permission for an underage marriage. The tension of that most heavy night of confession had remained unrelieved. I cannot think now of any time in my life when I have been more implacable. Although the real nature of my life remained mysterious to them, my parents did know something of me and realized hopelessly that were they to refuse me in this I would persist in some path that would seem true to me but perhaps even more disastrous to them.

Avalee and I sat close together, holding hands in the back seat. Her mother drove their lumbering old Dodge, a retired wide-finned police black-and-white, slowly across the great steaming valley. We entered the old river town from the east, rounded the empty afternoon streets, and pulled to a stop in the shade of ancient sycamores between the police department and the courthouse. I felt vaguely as if we were doing something not quite consonant with these old familiar buildings of civic propriety, with the sleepy, measured, leafy town they centered, baking the past hundred years in the valley sun. I felt a mixture of dim shyness and righteous defiance. Just as we stepped from the car, a large bulky man in uniform, puffing a cigar, emerged from the police station's brown doors and stepped toward the street beneath a cornice whereon was sculpted the form of an open book with the names Shakespeare and Emerson on either side. The police station had years before been built as a library. The big policeman darted a dark glance at us as he passed.

Now we marched slowly and without speaking across the courthouse lawn. I made sure I led the way, past the rusted cannon squatting on the grass. The courthouse loomed up before us, white, old, and authoritative. The date 1861 was imprinted in black on its front. In a show of support for the Old South it had been built in the ante-bellum style, and four massive Romanesque pillars framed the steps and door. A bronzed bear, looking somewhat like a small pig, graced the lintel.

We continued up the steps and through the doors, our footsteps echoing in the cool, wooden dark interior. A massive staircase mounted before us, but we turned to the counter of the court clerk. It was absolutely silent in the dim, ancient building. A scent of polish, tobacco smoke and wood paneling came from shadowed corners. No one else seemed about. My handwritten, unnotarized permission note was accepted without question or comment. It was a trusting and informal time and place even in such legal matters as this.

I do not know now if my memory of the judge who married us is real or simply composed of TV and movie characters, but real I think, all these country-judge caricatures having been based on just such a man as beamed upon us benevolently. Still holding hands, we allowed him to question us. We stood before him where he was enthroned behind an ornate desk in his office. There were many questions in his eyes, a hint of disapproval below his snowy mustache, a bit of a twinkle behind his gold spectacles. He asked us where we were from, recognized the towns and the families around the valley that Avalee and her mother mentioned, paid his respects to my father who had signed the note. As he was speaking, I looked at Avalee and was awed by her grace, maturity and womanhood. Her familiar girlishness had vanished here. I felt gawkily boyish beside her, skinny and insignificant before the judge. I was aware of what a curious spectacle we presented. "Well, this is a big step young man," he intoned. "A big, *big* step."

How can this possibly be a real marriage without this judge knowing anything about us? I thought. *Without the Buttes and the waterfall and my prayers and our tears in the cave and our love that came from God how can this make any sense to him?* "Well then." he resumed with a cough, "Too dark and official in this office for a marriage on a day like this. Follow me." And we obediently shuffled after him into the banistered walkway outside his third-story office. He led us to a tall-windowed balcony that overlooked the front courthouse lawn and the town block across the street. Opening the double-doors and stepping out a bit he said, "Out here…this will be better."

And so we were married there. I barely heard the judge muttering the incantation he knew so well. I felt the pressure of Avalee's hand slowly increase until it seemed she must be squeezing with all her strength. I felt the hot valley wind move and tuck around us like a blanket. I could smell her hair and her perfume beside me. I could smell Chinese food from Joe's Restaurant across the street and the fragrance of the farmland and forest from miles and miles beyond. I could see the steeple of the I.O.O.F hall between the trees. Beyond the streets the levee rose. Behind the levee the cottonwood trees quaked and murmured in the warm wind. Behind the trees just a sliver of the river shone. And far beyond the river, vague and barely hinted in the blue air, the brown parched visage of the Mountain gazed steadily at us, as here before the judge our love passed from that place of deepest dream out into the waking world. All uncertainty and timidity left me. *It doesn't matter at all if this judge or even if the whole world never understands what has happened to us,* I thought. And the judge said, "I now pronounce you man and wife."

I confess that boy as I was, I was well supplied with images of how things should be after two young lovers said marriage vows; images of a happy ride home together, family greetings and congratulations, an amber bedroom for love finally sanctioned by all. This was all to come later, but I was thinking of these things a little moodily as the black-and-white Dodge pulled to the side of the road just before the skeletal steel bridge spanned the river and I disembarked. Avalee and her mother must hurry on to Grandma's ranch in the foothills; this had been agreed. There was a little agony twisting in me at this, but Avalee quenched it with a smothering embrace and her lips close to my ear as she whispered, "I love you so much, so much. Just a couple of days! Bye!" She bounced back into the car and they were gone.

    The Buttes rose, clear and stark now over the painted green of the rice fields. My parents' house was on their farther side, and the empty highway narrowed to a shimmering, mirrored point. I was familiar and confident about hitchhiking in that broad safe countryside, but there were no vehicles just then and I began to walk. I was alone beneath the wide sky, companied only by the egrets and the redwings in the rice fields. I felt heavily the old valley-sense of spinning upon a great disk, circumference beyond vision. The Middle Mountain, as always happened when I stepped into its view, grasped my heart again like a vice. There was a slight sense of the valley floor tilting slowly like a vast magic carpet in flight. It would not take much for me to be pulled high into the air over river, forest and farm and into the Mountain, fixed at the hub of it all. On that highway alone, everything fell suddenly away. What had happened? Where were the deepness and firmness and utter rootedness of this joining of our lives? What did it mean that an hour after Avalee and I were married, I am walking alone through this blue and green empty loneliness again, only the Mountain and my Self seeming real? I remembered for an instant the wisp of web torn from the earth by the mountain's mystic wind, sailing away over us at the mouth of my cave. Where is she? My thoughts were unclear and my understanding here dim. As always, behind and beneath this opacity, the Mountain stood silently, the only thing needing no explanation. I walked on, now lifting my thumb as a few cars whizzed past.

Suddenly there is a threatening rumble close behind; a blast of exhaust and dust, the sound of big tires tearing the roadside gravel, and a very familiar, big battered green flatbed truck is lurching beside me. The handle is wrenched and the door kicked open. Tony's face grins below his sweaty hat. "Well! Hello there young man! Hop in!"

He says nothing for a minute or so while we drive east. Then, "Coming back from Williams. Got a load of alfalfa pellets. Got to stop up here in Meridian and get some groceries for my herders. Where you going?"

"Home," I answer. "On the other side of the Buttes."

The truck hums on. The levee rises into view dimly through Tony's dirt-caked windshield. I can see the Meridian drawbridge ahead. "Well young man…what have you been up to today? Where you been?"

There is a long pause while I think and swallow. There seems no reason why not to say, "I just got married…back at the courthouse."

"Ha! Well! You don't say!" There is another pause. "To that pretty girl you were with up in the Buttes at Bragg's cabin?"

"Yes," I feel deeply pleased now to tell him this. "Her name is Avalee. We're going to be together in a few days."

"But you're going to your folks' house now?"

"Yes, just for a few days."

"Huh." Another even longer pause. "Huh." Then, "Goddamn! Drawbridge is going up! Goddamn! Must be one of the last of those gas barges on the river here. I thought they were stopping those."

The great brown steel bridge, brittle and narrow, stands unnaturally almost upright before us. While we are stopped, I see the half-dozen little weedy streets of Meridian on the other side. A very modest-sized barge, equipped with two huge, oily tanks, comes pushed by a small shallow-bottomed tug, slowly up the river from the south. I had never had occasion to see commercial freight on the Sacramento River before, and was never to see it again. As Tony had guessed it may have been the last of its kind. Slowly and ponderously now, the bridge collapses, lights cease to flash, the gas tanker puffs upstream around a bend, and Tony, with a "Goddamn!" guns the flatbed truck down into town along Bridge Street. There doesn't seem to be more than thirty or so buildings in the whole town. Eric's Tavern here, painted a friendly, sulfurous red; the Methodist church there, with two rudimentary stain-glass doves in the window; a thin scattering of houses, a few standing venerable and Victorian between many more bungalows of indecipherable age and style. In the same way there still stand here and there, on corners and in yards, a few towering oaks of great and lovely age. Between these, and more numerous, are squashed and tortured shrubs and spindly trees of unsuccessful landscape varieties. There may be fifty or a hundred yards of old sidewalk, lifted and cracked into weedy concrete wafers.

  Tony pulls around the corner now to Third and Central, and the truck comes to rest before the Meridian Market. Without doubt this is the center and focus of town. The door is on the chamfered corner of the building, flanked by two twisted black walnut trees. The building is blanketed with a sheet-metal siding pressed to look like blocks, but the whole place is painted a deep green. Through the door I can see a bit of wood floor, and above that a ceiling fan slowly revolving. I immediately think of Coca-Cola. The place looks inviting.

Tony has put his hand on the door handle but now withdraws it. "Say," he says. "You ever mention that little idea of mine of making you a sheep-herder to your folks?"

"No," I answer a little morosely. "I never did."

"Good. Good thing. That was a crazy idea. Your girl had it right. Well, come on into the store and see what you'd be eating if you *had* become a sheep herder."

I doubt there were many florescent lights in Meridian California in 1964. The Sacramento Valley blazed so outside, that going into the store was like entering a comforting cave, lit by two yellow, bug-spotted bulbs hanging from the ceiling. A very old man in an apron stood behind the wooden counter. Sure enough, just before me was the large red and white sign that said, Things Go Better With Coke. The drink was flowing from an hourglass bottle into the smiling mouth of a curly-coiffed flapper. As Tony moved on between the shelves, I stood still in front of a large white cooler labeled Weber Refrigeration Made For The World-Wide Trade. It was full of very locally-made cheese and sausage and ground beef and big cuts of meat. The store was so small I could see Tony wherever he was. It was cool there and the slow, tired fan, suspended from a cream-colored sheet-metal ceiling pressed to an ornate parquet pattern, stirred the smell of cheese, bread, and dust, with just a hint of pigeon droppings mixed in. While I mused, Tony energetically grabbed items from the shelves all around and placed them on the counter. The old store-keeper began putting the groceries in boxes: long loaves of French bread, big bags of beans and rice, tortillas, a gallon can of tobacco and a pile of Zig-Zags, three gallon jugs of a deep red wine that reflected the light bulbs overhead with scarlet spots in the glass, lots of canned goods.

"That'll hold 'em for a couple of weeks," Tony said. "Well, thanks Howard, good day to you." The old man pulled a handle on the register, ripped off the tag and thrust it into his drawer.

The truck climbed the ramp onto the levee road and we curved slowly along the bending river under the cottonwood trees toward the Buttes. It is summer, too early for salmon or steelhead, but there are a few old guys out on the brown water, perhaps angling for sturgeon. I had seen a sturgeon once in the back of a pickup on the streets of Marysville. The end of the fish had drooped over the tailgate. There is a faint smell of fish and mud and weeds in the air near the river. The road leaves the levee and the river, past a great, gray, crumbling 1860's house, much too blasted to be inhabited, yet white and blue and red and brown flap in the slow breeze from a limp clothesline in the yard, and two dirty children are playing with a dog right in the road. Tony slows almost to a walking speed around the kids and the air suddenly seems wetter, heavier, thicker. Tules rise along the road all around. Over one more levee, and the truck plunges into the shadow of an oak forest bending over Butte Slough, a tributary waterway that seems absolutely motionless beneath the trees. On the bank, parked in the dirt, is a battered sedan, and a fat woman is sitting in a lawn chair watching her bobber. The flat bridge across the slough requires very slow going—fifty feet of crossbeams and two tire-tracks of twelve-inch planks. The water stews only a few inches below the wood. Mawson Bridge is strictly a low-water passage. On the right are the remains of an old steel bridge, chopped off at the east bank, frayed twists of rusty cable hanging limply toward the water, then a series of huge, upright concrete rectangles marching uselessly away between the oaks to end only a mile or so from the Buttes' southwestern rampart. The truck hums along the road through the wetland between the creek and the Buttes, through cool grass and twisted streams and park-like groves of oak bursting with health and life and shade, then turns abruptly toward the north, sweeps around the toe of a rampart ridge, up a long, rutted drive right to the Mountain's flank. We have come to rest before an old white house. "Old Wilbur Place," says Tony.

Just around the house, the door of a low bunkhouse opens and the two Basque fellows I remember from Bragg's Canyon come smiling forward, the dogs slinking around their heels. Receiving their provisions, they disappear. Sitting in the truck, I look more closely at the house. It seems to be of a similar vintage to my own boyhood home across the Buttes, but simpler, only one story. Instead of a detached tower rising behind as at home, here a second floor under a peaked roof had been built over just one small room, like a watchtower. There was no porch. There were three or four acacia trees in the yard, and a stone wall, made from andesite Buttes boulders, marked the yard.

As Tony returns and gets back into his seat behind the wheel, an old woman comes slowly into view around the house. She has tattered gray hair and is wearing a yellow bathrobe and slippers. She has a garden hose, and after waving her hand limply toward the truck, begins to shake the weakly dribbling hose at the tufts of dead grass in the yard. I notice now an old man sitting in the shadow of a tree, coughing and spitting toward his bare feet. "Old Bill and Milly Spease," says Tony simply. "He works sometimes taking readings off the gas wells. She tries to get a lawn going. I've rented to them for a long time. Fifty a month. They're getting too old to be this far out, so they are moving into town next month. Good thing, really. They've been hard on the house."

As we head down the drive, I am looking back through the window at the little box-like ranch house tiny against the soaring golden wall of the Mountain, the old people just spots against the whitewashed siding. Suddenly Tony stops the truck. "Say," he says, his voice pitched upward with sudden interest and friendliness, "say, have you and your new wife decided on a place to live yet?"

As I answer no, I realize suddenly I have not even thought about this in any specific way, but even before he has finished his sentence I feel a flutter of understanding and anticipation. "Well then! I could offer you youngsters this place! Forty dollars a month. Maybe you could help the old folks move and the first month'll be free. Otherwise it may take them half-a-year. It's not that pretty little cabin by the creek up under the cliffs back in the Buttes...but hey, second best!"

"Yes sir," I gulp. "Yes, this would be perfect for us!"

"Good." Tony starts the flatbed moving again and we bump and fume our way slowly through the dust. Then after a moment, "Good place. Nice old house out here in the Buttes...Bragg's Canyon just out your back door!" He winks. "You kids can live here as long as you want." He chuckles deeply. "Just don't stay too long or you might become another Milly and Bill."

Tony kindly offers to take me home. I know I will depart from him at some place away from the tall white house. I feel vaguely that I want him to think of me living with my sweet bride below the gazing Mountain, not as a schoolboy sleeping down the hall from my parents. He seems in a talkative, whimsical mood now, pointing out three or four ancient almond trees crouching, bare and barely alive, in the dry grass by the road. "Old Wilbur orchard," he says. He is wandering a little in his driving, obviously not taking the most direct route away from the Buttes. As we swing along West Butte Road to the south, the Long Bridge, an abandoned one-lane concrete span built in the 1930's but now an abandoned curiosity where locals walk to look below at the swirling high water, comes into view. Its eastern end laps onto the road at the base of the Mountain, and it crosses almost a mile of the wild wetland where the river overflows monstrously in winter. I know this place very well. Tony speaks my own thoughts when he says, "Maybe we'll get a look at old Jake the Walker." And sure enough, approaching the Long Bridge from the opposite direction comes Jake.

He walks bent, like a hunchback, but quickly. With each step he stabs the roadside with his stick. His head is completely bald, a ruddy brown, and a filthy red bandanna seems to be squeezing his neck. Over his back are slung two burlap sacks, and out of the top of one can be seen a shoot or two of something green. He is returning from some country store, probably Meridian, trying to sell flower bulbs. "Old Jake," murmurs Tony. "Lived under that bridge now more than thirty years."

I know this. I have spent many hours with that old man, listened to his hobo stories, how he hopped off the train nearby, sick of the car-load of aimless bums he was with, found the concrete maintenance shed under the east end of the old bridge empty and moved in never to leave again. "What a strange old duck," comments Tony as we pull along-side Jake the Walker. He beeps his horn as we pass and nothing changes with Jake except a quick, barely perceptible jerk of his brown head. "To live thataway under a goddamned bridge."

"His place is really pretty nice," I say hopefully. "I used to go out there and talk to him. He finds big pieces of glass and makes little hothouses and grows flower bulbs for the stores around here. He walks miles and miles. He has a little boat that he found when the water came up one year. He fishes. He has a nice little garden. He gets his drinking water from the Stohlman ranch across the road. Inside he has a stove with big turkey wings spread out over it. He has an old wind-up Victrola and about a thousand old records, music and comedy, all kinds. He sits and talks and talks and plays his records for me."

"Well I'll be goddamned," says Tony. "I didn't think that old man talked to anyone. He hasn't said ten words to me in ten years." Jake and the Long Bridge are far behind and we swing back onto Pass Road, ready to cut through this edge of the circular mountain cluster to the east. We bump along quietly for a moment. Outside, the flat, wet, green-forested valley has utterly disappeared, as if we had driven over the edge of one world into another—as indeed we have. Now the peaks of Middle Mountain tower on the left, its foothills on our right. Tony slows down almost to a stop as we pass the mouth of Brockman Canyon. His eyes seem to be searching there into the hazy, rocky distance. The sheep are all gone. The streams are stilled. The grass is tinder dry and the air is filled with bittersweet tarweed and roasting seeds. There is a merging in me now of the images of Brockman Canyon, the face of Avalee teasing me in our cave, her arms soon to be holding me in our bed in the Wilbur house, Tony and his life-long labor fully awake here in the middle of my dream, and Jake the Walker stopped once and for all at the Mountain's foot beneath his bridge like a taciturn, wise troll with many secrets.

"He told me it was really the Buttes that made him get off the train." My voice has dropped now to a tone of confidentiality. "He said something about how the Buttes made him feel really afraid and alone, rocky and high way out here alone in the middle of the valley, and really at home at the same time, but like they might trick him in some way. As if the Buttes had given him everything he needed here, but might take everything away from him also." I hesitated before adding, "Sometimes I feel that way too."

"Well I'll be goddamned," Tony grunted again.

We drive in silence over the pass, the tallest peak looming over us. The Mountain has stepped between me and everything else, and Avalee and the courthouse seem somehow far, far away. Tony turns the truck onto Butte House Road and the expansive, green tree-shaded cemetery appears, studded with tombstones, some tall and etched with time. There are a few fresh mounds here and there.

"Son," Tony says suddenly, "that old man Jake is crazy, that's why he lives under the bridge out there by the Buttes. He's not fit to live with other people. That's the *real* reason. And you should keep things like that to yourself. What do you think these people out here are going to think if you go on talking about their goddamn pasture like that?" Then he laughs brightly and reaches my knee with a gentle pat. "Now, tell me where to drop you off young man, and call me when you and your pretty new wife are ready to move in."

"Right here is good," I say after a mile or two. "I live right down the tracks here just an orchard or two away."

The green flatbed drones back toward the Mountain and I am walking down the railroad tracks toward the tall white house, balancing easily on one rail, my arms out like wings as I had done since I was a small boy. The day has waned and the tall trees in our jungled yard are suffused with the ambivalent glow of evening, the color of peaches ready for harvest. I creep into the yard to hide by the fishpond for a bit. The windows of the house glow and I can hear dishes clinking in the kitchen. Suddenly, my father bursts out of the back door and the screen slams behind him. I am sitting behind the little artificial mountain of Buttes boulders near the pond and cannot be seen. I wait until he has gone on down the walk, past the old tower and toward the barn. I am too late again to feed the horses and calves, and he is probably annoyed. I think of the courthouse, of the soft pressure of Avalee's hand, of the deliriousness of her scent, of the two of us as married, of Tony's words. Then I run quickly, before my father returns, up to the porch, scamper up the vent pipe and slip into my room among the tall whispering oaks to wait for the darkness.

***

Between the wide, defined sweep of the Sacramento River and the abrupt escarpment of the Buttes, fierce in contrast, a wide stretch of wetland and forest floods and pulsates in winter, steams and broods in summer. This is the Butte Sink, about 15 square miles full of deep swamp, primal grassland, twisted jungle creek, impenetrable groves of oak and vine with, in winter, a million ducks, geese and swans swirling above the shallow lagoons in sky-wide constellations of dizzy design and deafening song. The Middle Mountain's fifty square miles of crag, canyon, chasm, cliff and cove are the Sink's topographic opposite, but together they form the most unaltered wilderness of an ancient realm, the most unpunctured and undissected place in all the wide farm and urban lands of California's great Central Valley. Just the thin, cracking ribbon of old West Butte Road divides them, and here lived Avalee and Ira, just children really, but man and wife now, set down in their dream of love at the heart of the world.

From the front window or front yard of our old house, I occasionally looked westward to the flat, wet wilderness; but the western half of the house we left almost completely unoccupied and seldom stepped into the front yard. Most of the time my panoply was the upward sweep of the Middle Mountain just on the east side of the house. Avalee, in her boots and jeans with her flying hair and laughing wide eyes, played with her beloved horses in the corral between the house and the barn. She rode Little Buster, a funny, cantankerous, stocky palomino with a shock of forelock that stuck up like a brush, and I sat bareback on tall black Cassy as he loped along on spindly legs, usually lagging behind. We never saw anyone on our rides but occasionally old Sylvester, a mild, gentle-spoken odd old pioneer son who was our nearest neighbor, living alone in his collapsing house a mile away. He would break into a high, slightly crazy laugh when he saw us and wave as we passed. Together we often rode slowly up through Fig Tree Gulch and deep into Bragg's Canyon where we played in the grass and flowers, lay in the cool singing stream and chattered about babies, our great good fortune, and a rosy future. Sometimes we climbed to the cave and sat together silently.

That winter was one of the wettest on record, and after a week of heavy rain, the storm abruptly ceased, thick fog intervened, and while everything was still entirely soaked, a wall of 15-degree air froze the Buttes to a white, crystal silence. Every blade of grass, every leaf and twig, most of the stream itself, hushed and froze to a fuzzy, dazzling white. At nightfall the fog cleared and a full moon flooded this frozen landscape with heart-aching blue light. The Buttes, always a fairy tale come true, just shimmered in unbearable magic. Leaving the horses home, Avalee and I walked the miles slowly, too stunned to speak, to the frosty cabin in the night. I found some fairly dry twigs under a deep rocky cleft and we made a fire in the old stove. I pulled the rusty cot near the warmth, and while the owl, white as the frost and disturbed from the cabin rafters, circled and called in the cold, Christmasy silence, we lay quietly on the old cot for a long time before we walked slowly out of the deep Buttes wilderness back to the warmth of our house.

The old cabin was to burn to ashes soon, the canyon-bottom's biggest Blue Oaks would be poisoned to standing skeletons, and the meadow and stream to feel the bulldozer's blade soon after, but we never even guessed at such a thing.

Just in the dawn I would head out for work. My father, always encouraging, always giving even in the face of deep misgivings, had found just the right truck for us. It was a neat old '47 Dodge pickup, painted bright orange. It had a key and an ignition button, a pull-throttle, a wooden bed, a gun rack where I displayed an old single-shot twenty-two that Bill and Milly Spease had given me, and a scratchy radio with big digits on the dial. During this time in our dream we seemed to be little in the contemporary world outside, even somehow sucked into a pioneer past. However unlikely proclaimed by Avalee and Tony, I had become, after all, a sheepherder of sorts. In baggy pants, faded flannel and a big wide-brimmed droopy hat, I drove the orange Dodge to a nearby barn and loaded a half-dozen alfalfa bales and a sack or two of corn and bumped into a field where a thousand sheep began to gather toward me. The truck in gear, throttle pulled a little out, I would stand on the tailgate with a wire cutter and toss out flakes of hay, followed by streams of yellow corn, while the truck bumped, driver-less, slowly across the pasture. The old Dodge was a small truck so I did this over several times each morning. The ewes crowded around along the trails of feed, and I remember with delight how the lambs at these feedings would crowd together away from their munching mothers, separately in bunches of thirty or forty, and go bounding away in tight formation, leaping and twisting over the rocks in undulations of wool and joy. Sometimes I was gathering and pushing sheep across a mile of Butte Sink grass, or deep into familiar canyons and glens, humming and singing to myself. Sheep have curiously human voices and when I was all alone I sometimes could not resist standing on a rock and lecturing them. Shades of things to come. I won't recount my themes here, but the sheep would always, hundreds of them at a time, abruptly stop grazing, turn unanimously toward me, and with alert eyes and ears, listen carefully while they munched, grass and flowers sticking out of the corners of their green-stained mouths. I walked miles and miles of wire fences carrying baling-wire, pliers, hammer and u-nails and a wire twister, looking for breaks, tightening sagging lines. I even assisted with lamb "marking"—a term which generously describes only the sheep-dip branding part of the process. In the other part of "marking", I caught lambs and sacrificially held them up for quick, gruesome removal of tails and testicles. My boss was old-fashioned and with a flourish of a razor-sharp knife he sliced off the tail and the fuzzy end of the scrotum, and since the pink, exposed testicles were too slippery to grab, he gripped them in his teeth and ripped them out. "Wife kicks me out of bed during marking," he told me. This was a horror for me, but I bit my lip and did my job and after hobbling, crying and bleeding a little, the lambs would be jumping for joy the next morning, getting bigger and fatter, not of course to their ultimate advantage.

Sheep are relatively fragile as farm animals go, and these tiny, wobbly lambs even more so. In November during lambing, my boss put into my hands one of those long staffs surmounted with a metal hook and said, "Go on out in the field and git rid of the dead ones." So I wandered morosely through the maze of moaning, birthing ewes, stains and pools of afterbirth, healthy new lambs enthusiastically nursing, and looked for the dead ones, lying like dirty scraps of debris here and there. I pulled these little corpses toward me with the crook and then grasping as many bony little legs as I could gather in hand, toted this dismal cargo to a far corner of the field and stacked them in a pile that grew higher each morning. *A Pile of Dead Lambs.* The phrase seemed like the title of a story or a poem. Every now and then some confused and forlorn ewe would follow me for a short while, sniffing and bawling. The vultures worked steadily on these dead piles, skinny coyotes would occasionally sneak up and drag a withered little corpse away, but when the scavengers couldn't keep up with the death rate, my boss would burn the stack and for awhile the mild, rustic eclogue of the sheep ranch would be clouded with a nasty stink.

One afternoon I rescued a little "bummer" lamb, a surprisingly hardy little guy who had not only lost his mother, but had somehow escaped the traditional surgery as well. Avalee scooped him up and nurtured him until he was a husky young critter with, if possible for a sheep, a wild look in his eye. He utterly rejected the normal ovine destiny and one morning he made a run for it and escaped over the rampart and into the chaparral. It was amazing how fast and desperate was his flight into the high rocks, his long uncut tail waving like a woolly banner as he ran. Avalee was deeply gratified by the thought of this renegade's wild freedom. Whenever we met old Sylvester on one of our rides he would screech, "Hey hey you youngsters!! Saw that crazy long-tailed buck-sheep of yers gallivanting up in the rocks like a deer! Ha!" Old Sylvester liked sheep as individuals and had names for all of his own, and it was clear that somehow he viewed that wild lamb that Avalee had raised as a triumph of sorts.

In the evening I would swing the old Dodge into our driveway, home for the night after earning all of eight dollars for the day's labor. I never went into the front door of the house. There was a very small back mudroom, and while taking off my boots and dirty hat, the smell of greasy paint on old walls, century-old floors, wood smoke from the stove, or gas from the ticking and groaning old heater made me feel at home. The mingled aroma of rice and beans bubbling on the stove would make me immediately hungry. Avalee was a good and energetic housekeeper, even if we lived in only three rooms, furnished so little and simply that little need be done but keep the weed-chaff and dust from just outside off floor and tabletop. The old house, loosened in all of its parts by a hundred seasons of wind, wet from the south, dry from the north, had long since surrendered its seal and most of it was too drafty to keep warm. From the main side entrance a hallway divided the structure into two parts. Two large rooms off that hall to the left we kept closed, cold and empty. Two rooms to hall's right we kept soft with warmth even in the coldest winters. One was the kitchen, inhabited by a brown-stained refrigerator rounded on top and embellished with rusty chrome strips down the door's center, a really huge old antique of a gas range, and our little round kitchen table. All of this, appliances and furniture, would never surrender its patina, however much we scrubbed. Rice, beans, oatmeal, toast, coffee, popcorn; these are things I recall smelling, wonderfully cooking there in the kitchen. One evening we answered a timid knock at the back door, and there was Manuel, smiling and holding out to me a small bag of "rocky mountain oysters", as they are called. "For you and wife," he said. "Fry 'em up! Very good!" It was a generous and friendly gesture since I knew Manuel and Jess prized these dubious little nuggets, but I thanked him and put them aside. Lamb testicles were not on our menu.

The other room, adjacent and what I suppose was designed as a dining area, is where we huddled near the stove, watched the single station we received on a tiny black and white TV, eating popcorn during long dark evenings. At the end of the hall was the bathroom, warmed only by a hazardous little electric heater on the floor by the tub. Through the door from the dining room was the bedroom, almost always closed and dark. We didn't try to keep it warm very often. When we were in there, we were deep in bed, intertwined and breathing each other in beneath mounds of blankets, to the rattle and song of the Middle Mountain rains dashing against the house.

And before very long our single brand-new bit of furnishing is added; a white baby-crib over which Avalee has poured all of the textile grace and loveliness we can muster. Our tiny baby boy sleeps there, at the foot of our bed in warmer months, just outside the door in the warmer room during winter. I often lay awake deep into those rainy, whispering nights, listening to the child's snuffles and murmurs, listening to his mother's soft, even breathing. Who are we now? Are we very different from those two lovers in a dream, child-lovers playing together in the bright light of a vision, in the hidden wonder of our magic mountain, in the unmatched tenderness of our mountain cave? Just what is the difference between that life and this? Is there a difference at all? Is anything lost of the dream as we wake into the world? Is the world around the Mountain also the dream?

About this time, in the fecund garden of these night-musings would sometimes begin to germinate a sort of gnawing inspiration for creative confession. I was not thinking of this in any rational, deliberate way, but I began, in those nights, to have a sense that this emergence of my secret, intimate world of Middle Mountain dream and love, into the working, waking, domestic world, was connected to a story that I must tell beyond myself. And so often now I would slip from bed and creep up the shallow stairs to that one second story room that rose above the low-roofed house. Here in the empty cold, I would sit before the eastern window where I could see the Buttes glowing on moonlit nights, and leaning over a dusty table, I would write,

write, write, feverishly. In the raw, florid, naïve language and cadence of my 18 years I was trying to find a way to press the Mountain into a media. I saw it as a film and I wrote; *The big white house suddenly opened its eyes, as the light in each window flicked on, like a large snowy owl welcoming the darkness. Warmth streamed from the glowing windows and dim beams of light stretched across the lawn. A door opened...slammed. The figure of a young man walked slowly through the mist and out of the gate.* A tortured young man was to conquer disillusion within the sacred mountain. *Far beyond the range of city sound, far beyond the reach of searchlights and streetlights, the jagged hills lay in silent blackness. Soundless they were not, for through the leafy canyons and gorges a dainty breeze crept, stirring cottonwood leaves into an invisible dance and an audible song,* I wrote. The poor young man was staggering blindly from a heartbreak into the waiting arms of the Mountain. *With head buried in his arms, the boy hovered beneath the nearby oaks. With eyes tightly closed and mind equally shut he drifted into a sleep designed to shut out the shattered pieces of memory that jutted before his consciousness. In the face of bitter disillusion, something beneath his soul had led him to places of solitude and quiet, and although he was unmindful of them, a thousand hills nodded welcome and winds whispered their hellos through the shifting locks of a thousand trees...*and so on and so forth. I revived my old, crushed dream a little in this midnight script; *...by the time the last remnant of light had left the sky, new shingles had been nailed upon the roof and the door hung solidly on two strong hinges. Inside, blankets had been stretched across the ancient bunk. The cold rusty iron of the stove in the corner was warmed by a crackly fire and from the crumbling chimney a spiral of gray smoke drifted into the wind and was whisked away over the hilltops.* Ultimately the tortured young man finds his foolishness, if not his inner prolixity, somewhat subdued by a new, ecstatic vision of the world. *Here is sanctity which shames your religions, and reality which discredits your heroes and your saints. Here you find the circumstance which dwarfs every other* *circumstance and the standard by which every creature is judged. Oh man, on your knees and give thanks, and let your reverence consume your being, for your body is within the cathedral of the universe. Let your heart enter in also.*

It was a pagan vision of the mountain, to be sure, but how evangelistic also! As I wrote this, I imagined being able somehow to film it all and present it to great, appreciative audiences. Although I had written a good deal since early childhood, stories and raptures of all kinds, never before this had I conceptualized bringing the power of media to bear on the wonder of the Mountain. Writing alone in that little tower room I was grandly shaken...and deeply disquieted.

Disquieted as is the dreamer feeling the vision passing across his eyes like water when the swimmer rises to the bright blue. Disquieted in the same way I had been when first daring to take Avalee to most secret, sacred places. Disquieted because many things were changing, and I was no longer a child, no longer a boy, but now a man with wife and babies, feeling the full force of human life impelling him along. I wrote and wrote. I became enamored of the technical tools of story telling, seduced by the magic of media. I had no stories but one, but that one I was preparing myself to tell, and I wrote and wrote. A boy could be a sheepherder but a man could not, and I became a radio announcer at a tiny AM station in town and as I disc-jockeyed, sang along with Tommy James and the Shandels—*crystal blue persuasion!*... and Dion—*has anybody here seen my friend John?*... and Marvin Gaye assuring me—*ain't nothin like the real thing baby!* I broadcast the news, "ripped from the wires of the Associated Press", of Viet Nam and other scenes of assassination. We exchanged the old orange pickup for an almost new little green Volkswagen Bug and prepared to leave the old farmhouse rental at the foot of the Buttes' pale green rampart, for our own first home across the river.

One afternoon a day or two before our actual departure, I left the piles of boxes and the disrupted house, which seemed to sulk as it waited for another abandonment. Tony waved as he passed me where I was walking up the rampart hill near the house, and I waved back in the cloud of dust his old truck left. He approved of our moving. We were not to become another Bill and Milly, he said, no sir.

Without knowing why, I had grabbed the old single-shot twenty-two from the back mudroom and was carrying it with me toward Brockman Canyon. I had one shell in my pocket. I was only one of the countless boys and men who had, before me, walked armed to kill into the Middle Mountain, but I had no thought of this at all, being no hunter, never having even target-practiced before. There was some unarticulated image playing deep in me that I was acting out with my boots and this rich spring day and this gun, and I really did not think about it at all. In an hour's walk past Goat Rocks and Lover's Leap, I was following Brockman Creek, now almost silent and dry, passing the huge mossy boulders where I had, years ago, rested once before the white deer had led me to wonder and confusion. A hundred yards beyond, and I was climbing a region of downy hills, folded like loaves of bread. The leaves of the oaks all around were stiff and rattled just a very little in a breeze too light to really feel. I rounded the hilltop. Suddenly, far below, I saw just the tips of two long bifurcating ears almost at the bottom of the high hill near a wire fence, nearly a hundred yards away, into the sun. It was a thing just barely seen. I had no thought whatsoever of actually doing harm to the jackrabbit waiting breathlessly there below. It was an utterly impossible shot and I had only fired the gun once before at a can, and widely missed. I didn't like firing the gun at all, really. But in the same automatic way I had picked up the rifle, in the same way I had strode out to the canyon, in that same way I raised the sight to my eye, paused not even to renew my glimpse of the ears, and pulled the trigger. The crack, echoing off the high cliffs, made the breeze and my heart stop short and I saw something leap way down below, through the shinning grass. "He is charging away, scared by the shot, way over the other hill by now," I thought, and I continued at a slow pace down toward the fence. But he had not charged away. In utter shock, I saw that somehow, inexplicably, that random bullet had found its way to his little heart and his leap had been a last leap of death. The creature, unspeakably warm, soft, limp, beautiful and spotted with blood, lay still in the faded flowers. And I cried as I took him toward the creek, and I prayed and asked his forgiveness as I buried him beneath a manzanita. I had never in all my life harmed any living creature before. It is clear why I have remembered this, for many reasons, but the most pronounced is that in that moment, I grasped intellectually for the first time what this place of rock and tender hardness was doing in my life, how everything I was learning and knowing seemed to somehow come pouring out with the Mountain's eruption through the gentle plain of my life. But this sudden stark knowledge notwithstanding I had no idea why I had done this murderous thing and I was lost in confusion. I walked slowly back to the house to continue packing and I never told a living soul of this event—until I told it to you just now. It is a time for telling secrets.

So our boxes and sticks of furniture were carried around the western flank of the Buttes to Pass Road, then eastward past the village of Sutter and its broad manicured cemetery, past my parents' big white house nesting in the tight grove of huge trees in the middle of the orchards, through Yuba City, Marysville and Olivehust, across the river to a tidy ranch house, almost new, with fifteen acres of irrigated pasture and a little white barn.

This was the first time Avalee and I had conducted any significant part of our conjoined lives apart from the Middle Mountain, but we consoled ourselves with the inevitable, jagged, familiar form that rose over the Feather River, just at the end of our drive and across the field. We usually woke up very early and followed a happy routine. She and I walked together in the wet pasture grass behind the house, moving sprinkler pipes for the day's irrigation while the kids played around us. When there was time before I must head to work at the little radio station, we walked up the levee where through the cottonwoods, quiet and still in the morning mist, we could watch the slow, brown swirling of the river and see the Buttes beckoning to us just a few miles away to the west.

But it seemed also that we were at the Buttes almost as often as we were at the new house. Every available afternoon we carried our toddlers into the folds of Brockman Canyon or visited for awhile with gentle old Johnny Myers and his cranky but kindly wife, until they sent us strolling from their timeless kitchen up the creek with a bag of her cookies to Peace Valley, where the little boys played, dropping with their tiny new hands, the prettiest pebbles they could find into the deep, ancient streamside mortars. Their mother, laughing, singing and scolding with them as she had with me when we were nearly children ourselves, was more a beautiful fairy to me than ever before. Those long, meditative mountain wanderings during which our love had germinated and flowered, were hardly possible now with the constraints of time and children, but we had very secret nooks, easy to reach, where the whole Being of the mountain resided powerfully in tiny shrines of a few rocks, a single tree, a four-foot patch of creek bed. These visits, these compulsory homecomings, were the pure substance, the nectar within which floated and bobbed the more ambivalent activities of our practical life routines and ambitions.

We were becoming naïve but boundlessly hopeful young entrepreneurs. In an available space within the radio station where I was employed, we had arranged to begin building our own sound and film production studio where I intended to turn out all sorts of masterpieces, the first of which was to be my film-story of the tortured and ecstatic young man in his magic mountain. I did not really attempt to consider it then, but I know I felt the subtle tension of this divergence; our dream of contentment in the Mountain, and our descent to the valley, where we might sing the dream widely in the world. Whatever these subtle and unexamined feelings, I resisted the separation of these aspects of life, partly by unremitting devotion to our regular Buttes pilgrimages. Almost always when we drove over the rivers to work on the studio, we continued after work, on a few more miles westward, and played, dreamed and worshipped in the Mountain as we always had done.

Like that very special, soft, warm morning in August.

When we reached the end of the gravel drive and turned north to skirt the levee along Feather River Boulevard Avalee said, "I have an idea. Let's skip the work until later this afternoon. It'll be cooler up in the Buttes in the morning. We can take the boys to that place in the creek-bed between those two big boulders and they can play in the sand. You remember that place." She smiled mischievously at me with a provocative sidelong glance. "The dry moss and the grape vines smell good there in the morning." The little green car whined along between the irrigated peach trees and the dense and thriving yellow of mustard. The little boys squealed and squabbled in the back seat. "Mommy," the four-year-old said in his little voice, "can we climb up the mountain and play in the cave?"

"Why sure, my little man," Avalee said, as she reached over the seat and ruffled his hair. "You can carry your little brother up there!"

"He's too big and heavy and his legs drag in the weeds and he gets stickers and he cries. Daddy can carry him. Can we make a fire and roast weenies?"

"We can't have any fires in the Buttes when the grass is dry," I say sagely. "We'll save the climbing for the winter and stay down in the cool places today. It will be nice."

"Oh shoots!" the child replies.

"Yea, shoots," repeats the little one. Avalee smiles and says, "You can look for shiny rocks and see the magpies. It will be lots of fun, even if we don't climb up to the cave." Just then, as we pass the four-way stop and the shabby country store, two of the yellow-billed flashy birds hop away from a squashed rabbit in the road.

The bridge over the Yuba and into old-town Marysville looms ahead. It arches high over the Gold Rush river, unlike the older, narrow, flat span with its ornamental concrete railing. When the old bridge had been demolished to make way for its wider, sterile replacement, mysterious brick tunnels were found leading from the river toward the Gold Rush-era streets of Marysville. There had been, at the time, inevitable talk of a Chinese underground, although no one mentioned the probably more plausible explanation of sewers and storm-drainage. I, of course, didn't think of such things either, and as a boy I had written a fantastic little mystery novel about smuggling and paddle-wheeled steamers and shanghaied drifters. As we began to ascend the arch of the bridge the Buttes came just barely into view and Avalee said in a quiet voice, "I miss the old Wilbur

Place. Sometimes I think the old board walls and the Buttes right by the back door were better than the new house with its' air-conditioning."

"Well," I said, "let's move back!"

As we ascend the bridge, the details of Olivehust's garish mess are obscured from view behind us. The tall, conspicuous steeple of Saint Joseph's rises at the center of the graceful old 1850's town. I had often visited that old church and had self-consciously taken note of the inscription, quoted from the second chapter of Luke, engraved over the high doors: **"His mother then said to him, son, why hast thou done so to us? Behold, thy father and I have sought thee sorrowing."** At the apex of the bridge's arch, the forest-lined river seems to bear little mark of the 1960's and just beyond, appearing magically behind the river trees against the pale summer sky, the serrated form of the Middle Mountain takes its place as the absolute center-piece of the whole landscape: rivers, serpentine riparian forest, the twin towns grown from the craze for gold, the religious icon of Saint Joseph's, the broad and rich California farmland beyond crowded with agricultural abundance. The Mountain anchors it all.

"Maybe we *should* move back to the Buttes," Avalee says wistfully as the Mountain rises into view. "Maybe moving over here was a mistake." Now we descend the bridge toward the streets of the town, and as we loose our elevation, the river and the Mountain disappear behind the tangle of the traffic, the streetlights and concrete and the new Mervins, built where a portion of Old Town was bulldozed.

We are going to take our usual shortcut past the grotesque construction of the Tahitian Motel, through the back streets, past the emergency entrance of the hospital, toward the obsolete train depot on the levee, then over another older river-crossing to Bridge Street, out of the clutter and into the familiar Buttes countryside. "Oh well," Avalee says, "more dreams." As we stop at the light waiting to make our left turn, she turns toward me to settle the little boys securely in their seats. Her bright auburn hair falls over her cheek as her gentle, slender hands reach for her children. I think of our destination deep in the quiet canyon of the Buttes, and an unspeakable sense of my love for her presence floods over me.

Then, utterly disconnected and unrelated to anything and everything about us that mellow morning, there is an explosion, like a bomb detonating in the little green car. In the midst of the shriek of tearing and grinding metal, I am floating in a strange, almost poetically slow crystalline mist of disintegrated glass that seems suspended in the air. Avalee's face is tilted gracefully to one side, under the roof crushed only on her side of the car, and from somewhere around her head has erupted a fine red rain of blood that floats before me atomized in the jewel-like, suspended shards of glass. I see the children, their little faces frozen in a dreamy expression of wonder, eyes wide and staring, tumbling in the air behind me, and it all is happening like a slow ballet. I am dimly aware that a large truck has fallen, seemingly from the sky onto our little car, and is grinding it, like a crushed tin can under a great, steel heel, across the intersection where it finally and suddenly comes to a complete stop. After the deafening rage of the collision, this is now happening very quietly, and we have come to rest in the squashed Volkswagen in a complete and eerie silence. Avalee is leaning toward me, her head resting on my shoulder. She seems unmarked, her hair barely out of place, her face serene. She looks very beautiful, her eyes closed as if sleeping, dreaming a peaceful dream, and I simply want to gently wake her up. "Avalee," I murmur, "are you OK?"

As I speak to her, I cradle her face in my hands and feel the familiar warm, moist softness of her skin. So very gently, I tilt her face upward from my shoulder, and as I do this, blood flows suddenly from between her parted lips and over my hands. There is a sudden image of her face and red spring flowers on a green hillside. Still I hold her warm face in my hands and am dimly aware of frantic bystanders lifting the little boys, crying but seemingly unhurt, from the floor behind the back seats. Chaos fills the street all around. An ambulance shrieks. Police-car lights flash and gyrate. Someone nearby lies on the street and wails. Bystanders are attempting to rock the ponderous old truck, leaning at an ungainly angle, off of the mangled mass of metal in which we sit, frozen in immobility. The children and I seem unharmed, and the little boys are gently lifted through the open doors of the car, as their rescuers, crying out themselves, rush about to extract the babies from the little fragile, crushed car. But in the midst of this scene of frantic destruction, I continue to sit in absolute stillness, still holding her auburn head between my hands, pondering her quiet face and feeling her blood flow from her mouth and run slowly over my hand, down my arm, dripping into her lap from my elbow. And Avalee, my love, my mountain love, also is absolutely silent, still, as if content, slightly smiling, quietly and suddenly dead.

VI

A son distracted by the voices of passionate spirits is a poor choice to count the tears his mother has shed for his life, but I can remember now only two times I heard my mother wail and weep for me. First, muffled through the walls during the long night of my disclosure of Avalee's pregnancy, and then echoing down the hospital halls at the doctor's toneless disclosure that her son's beautiful young wife had been already dead when the ambulance brought her from the wreck. While I had ridden with her in the back of the ambulance, watching the two faceless attendants fiddling around her, watching her body shift limply with the vehicle's movements, I had asked, "Is she breathing?" "We're doing everything we can," one of them had muttered. I knew then. Now I could hear my mother's wails from where I lingered near the open door of the trauma room. I could see from there the starched edges of the doctors' smocks and hear the mutterings of emergency nurses. I knew from the tones of their half-whispered speech what they were saying. And just visible past the scuffed, scrubbed and sterile door frame, I could see the bottoms of Avalee's jeans and her old boots from her knees downward, still a little muddy and grass-stained from the pasture, drooping limply outward on the gurney. I could see the soft palm of her hand lying near her knee, tipped upward toward the light.

I had left her lying dead in that sterile hall and had lain stunned on my old four-poster bed, not even able to think. Now much later in the moonless nightmare dark of that night, the rubble of the empty creek bed that led from the valley's fruited garden into the parched muddle of these dead volcanoes, tripped and twisted my feet. Sometimes I stumbled in the rocks; sometimes I crawled. I was weak with weeping and there was a sickening pain in the vessels and tissues of my brain. But even in this utter illness of soul and body, I was being drawn to creep in the night, helplessly whipped along like a dog, deep into the Mountain. I felt like some sort of worm slithering into the gut of that place. But all of the world was empty of any other destination, and finally, as I made my way across the flatness that someone had perversely, as it seemed now, named "Peace Valley", the high claw of Cat Rock rose very dimly in the dense sky like a black lie.

In an otherwise empty mind, I could actually hear her voice, bubbling, lilting, serious and sweet, imploring and naively insistent. The girlish tone of her speech was not memory. It was present sound, heard clearly in my ears, soft in the rustle of parched grass, smooth in the rattle of the thistles and the dried husks emptied of their seeds.

"*I think you are making this all up, little mountain boy,*" she said again.

"It's because you don't like it when anybody tells you your dreams are just dreams and maybe you shouldn't take them so seriously," she said again.

"I really do love your stories and your dreams most of the time, but you know there is a difference between the things we imagine and make up and the things that are really true in the world," she said again.

And finally, *"Oh well, more dreams,"* I heard her say again, just before that mass of rusted metal had fallen upon her from the sky.

Cat Rock, like a huge piece of broken glass stuck vertically into the soft and rounded sedimentary beds at the head of Peace Valley, has a hidden crack in its topmost point through which we had often squeezed to cling together in the chill and watch Venus rise in the blush of dawn, like a celestial ornament at the very peak of North Butte. It has an anciently inhabited smoothly rounded cave at the talus – cliff boundary where we had often slept. And hidden behind Cat Rock's crystalline aciculae, it has a huge stone seat so like a throne it looks as if it has been hewn, where I used to sit with a deliberately pompous, foolish posture while she laughed and teased me and made jokes about 'the little king of the mountain sitting on his molehill.' Where the vertical cliff meets its supporting, steep-sided cone, the brushy slope falls away steeply until its sheerness is attenuated just enough to hold some lovely bedrock mortars under a few dwarfed bonsai oaks overlooking a flat meadow. Right out in the center of the meadow is a chunk of gray porphyry the size of a dining-room table and just as flat, two or three feet higher than the grass. It would have been perfect for acorn pounding, even better than the mortars above, being much smoother and a hundred yards closer to the creek. But there are no rounded mortar holes on that table rock, indeed very little roughness of any kind. I have no doubt this absence of mortars, this polished smoothness, is deliberate. Was it indeed a feasting table? Or a place of prayer? Or an altar of sacrifice? Or a dolmen of healing?

After a day of sunshine in any season, the table rock soaks and stores warmth like a battery, and long into a chill night will warm a body pressed to it with the comforting magic of heated stone. Of all places in the world on that sickened night, this was where I needed to be, and stumbling across the meadow onto this rock, I fell, thinking of nothing, exhausted and damaged as never before in my little life. I had by this time been wrung dry of tears like a soiled and twisted rag.

On through the empty night I lay there paralyzed, vacant and thoughtless. There was no wind. The doomed cattle out in the moonless night had hushed their normal midnight mourning. The only sound was an unidentifiable wail, repeated over and over like a chant, the strange song of some wild creature making sounds far outside its known repertoire, as people who wander in the night know they sometimes do.

I never noticed the beginning of the dawn, and consciousness was only a thick, stupid pain. But there was something coming up from the Mountain, up through the rock, seeping into my limbs, guts and head like the hoarded heat of the stone. It was a *seeping in* that had nothing to do with any intention of mine, an indifferent capillarity, cruel now, like the insistent rasping of a body scalded of its skin.

You will not leave me alone even after this. This whimper was the first beginning of a thought within me. The blanket of the cool dark night was being roughly pulled away. As day insisted itself over the night, the August heat gradually made the night-warm table rock into a griddle. And when the whimper hardened into a thought it was her voice again: *There is a difference between the things we imagine and make up and the things that are really true in this world.*

She had been *so sure*, in her gentle insistent way, that her sweet, trusting life in the world of her Lord's keeping was the Real, while my pretty perception of stone as tender spirit was only an endearing fancy. She had never wavered in asserting this whenever I brought my ghostly mountain-dreams before her. And despite my protests, I had begun to believe her in some way, to fit these convictions of hers into my understanding, because I knew that her materialization in my mountain-life was part of the Place's revelation, to which I seemed forever forced to heed. Now these 'fancied' spirits of the stones remained most certainly, present all around me, whispering harshly in my ears; and she, whose body and spirit I had thought were as permanent as earth itself, was gone.

So even while stricken unimaginably in the foolish, helpless tenderness of youth, I was being jerked forcefully into the way of a deep enigma that oozed into even that oblivion as a wordless sense: *How could the Mountain's mass express the transcendence of matter, as I knew it did? What did this place mean? What was this Mystery it was so ruthlessly pressing upon me?* And how could just dawdling here possibly be enough now?

This was the dilemma that seeped into me, gradually, insidiously, in the midst of ignorant agony and black betrayal. It must have been because reflexively, I knew that the idiocy of her destruction must somehow be explained by the miracle of the Mountain's creation. This excruciating riddle had been injected into me with the piercing ease of a hypodermic, but any will—or indeed, ability—to address it had been smothered by the sheer weight of grief and confusion. Or perhaps had, through some indulgence of that jagged-headed master, been mercifully withheld.

Withheld while I wandered for awhile. I tried to get far away, driving rather blindly north into the forested foreign dark of British Columbia until the pavement ended near some place called Horse Tail Creek, and a washboard road rattled the car to a stupid halt where I abruptly turned around and headed south. Or far to the opposite southeast of home, to the superstitious, tattered desert around Roswell New Mexico, and then even farther into the dirty alleys of Juarez. This was all a futility, as I knew as I fled, and there was only one place I could be.

So I returned quickly, but stayed, I thought, just out of reach of the Mountain, while keeping it always in view. There were nights of drifting about the streets of the college town just north of the Buttes, fragrant as only a small, Sacramento Valley town can be, nestled in a forest of creek-side oaks, old houses and ancient street trees, encompassed by square miles of ripening orchard and stewing rice field. There were sleepless nights and nights in musty back-shed blankets behind old rented houses, warmed by the unqualified welcome of small tribes of the young bohemians of that day, pervasive, sweet and dreamy like the smoke and music that filled the houses.

And thus during these wanderings, I began to remember what I had sensed the morning after that black night on the baking flat table beneath Cat Rock; that simple, childish, dazzled dawdling in the Middle Mountain was for me no longer enough; that in the alluring loveliness of its form was embedded an inevitable mystery, and that my life could offer no alternative but trying relentlessly to find it out. I had been, without much mercy it seemed, cast out of the cradle, and felt my grown-up feet firmly on this mountain path. And although quite compelled to walk it, I could not see quite where it led.

My ragged old backpack was gradually being filled with various items from the Cohasset Curio shop, a small comfortable rattletrap old house teetering beside the foothill road not far from the pavement's end. It was an unassuming little junk shop filled from floor to ceiling, shelf upon shelf, with wonderful useful stuff. Cohasset Ridge, Musty Buck Ridge, Stilson Ridge, these and many others were the ridges dividing the streams flowing to the Sacramento River, stretching themselves onto the valley from the Cascade Range north and east of the Middle Mountain, like fingers pointing out its strange fifty mile isolation in the flatness. I could see the Buttes from the dirty back window of the shop.

But I was looking for a metal plate. Here was one, once white enamel over pewter, chipped but perfect, sitting on a shelf with a lot of kitchen stuff from some old vanished cabin in the woods nearby. I found a similar tin cup. I grabbed an old tarnished spoon, knife and fork. A small burnt grill. A wooden cooking spoon with a long handle. An army surplus collapsible shovel and a very small ax. A brown dish towel. Later some oatmeal, beans, coffee and dried bread. All of this was packed. I was ready.

Somewhere back in an interior canyon, the most spectacular cottonwood tree in the Middle Mountain rises a hundred feet out of the rocky dark deepness. In summer this huge tree whispers, hypnotically whispers, almost without ceasing. In the fall, a million little puff-seed fairies float around its head. In the stark leafless winter, its branches look huge, smooth and ornamentally white. The trunk near its base is much too large to reach around and the deep gray bark can barely be seen beneath a twisted lattice of grapevine, each snake-like, clinging portion as big around as a child's arm. These vines can be climbed if one can tolerate the ants. And right at this tree's knees is a yard-wide pool, never dry winter and summer and months between, and if you look closely into that black mirror you will see some things. You will see perfect little fingers of water streaming in from the mossy bank. And if the light is just right you will see, at certain times, the reflection of a hundred vultures hunkered high, high above in the white branches of the tree, like black ornaments, and they are looking out thinking of dead things, and they are looking down watching you. I would lie by the pool, and as hours passed, watch the huge graceful birds return from their wide wandering to settle, one by one, in the high branches of the great tree. One afternoon I counted them; one hundred twelve large black birds, some crouched, some holding wings wide spread as if ready for flight (or airing their underarms, as I sometimes whimsically mused), but every one silent and motionless. If you want to sleep beneath a hundred roosting vultures, it is a good idea to have a canopy of some kind over you. I excavated a small dug-out in the soft, pungent humus, about the size and shape of a shallow grave, covered it with a dense lattice of bay boughs and leaves, and carefully covered it again with the soil and leaves dug from the depression. I was protected from the pungent white droppings of the vultures, surprisingly inoffensive and not at all as smelly as one would expect, and also comforted and embraced by the earth itself, like a tiny, vulnerable burrowing creature in his invisible den. Someone passing through that glen would never have seen me. Safely beneath this tree, hidden entirely, I slept and dreamed of death.

She and I are holding each other tightly, but we are slowly swirling, spinning in a brown maelstrom like a tornado, and as our spinning quickens, we begin to be torn apart, and we are crying to each other as this centrifugal force separates us, and I spin off alone into blackness.

This dream sharply awakened me as it always did. I climbed out of the cottonwood's lair and moved through twisted oaks back out to the very edge of the wide grass. It was one of those forgotten, unconscious night-spent hours before the dawn and the full moon was still glowing across the little valley before blinking out behind a black hill. In that light the grassy openness was almost white, but out there not a hundred yards from where I sat, was a large black stain. This was a crematory open to the staring sky. Here, not long before, the cattleman had hitched a chain to the stiff leg of a steer's carcass and with his pickup had dragged the corpse into the open and set it afire. I didn't understand why. This was just the sort of thing that black-feathered, redheaded crowd in the cottonwood would have noticed and taken care of quickly. But I had seen it done from behind a high rock.

Now in the distance to my right and left, I heard the moaning of the range cattle, and they began to emerge from the black beyond into the moonlight, from here, from there, shuffling along slowly, moaning deeply, forming lines. They marched out toward the black stain, and there, falling silent, they formed a circle, standing shoulder to shoulder around the oily spot with its blackened bones, and stood in some kind of ceremony of recognition. *These beeves, this meat, these doomed walking dead things; these stupid dim cattle* were doing this. They stood quietly perhaps five minutes, then turning slowly, they moved back again into the black margins of the night, moaning as they vanished. I told this story once to a cattleman I will not name, and he laughed at me with a sick smile on his face.

Awakened from a dream of death, I had stumbled on a scene of death. Now as the spring sunshine began warming the mountain that held me, I thought, for relief, of a clear pool below a little waterfall where the stream fell down the terraces of a sharp canyon. By the time the sun was warmly overhead, I was sitting under the waterfall on golden sand beneath silver water. I let myself feel cleansed of what I had dreamed and watched in the night. Barefoot, I followed the cascade downstream past the brightness of wildflowers. My eyes were on the water and the shimmer of beautiful stones. Then I nearly stumbled on the bloated mound of brown that was a dead cow, lying directly in the stream, waters dividing around the huge corpse. The glistening body of her calf, only half-emerged from the womb, dead in the very midst of birth, was wavering like a suggestion beneath the current. I stood there on the bank for a very long time, stunned, staring, pondering. *Wombs and tombs, wombs and tombs,* revolved in my mind like a dirge. Right in the midst of the exquisite gush of spring, the Mountain was flinging this in my face wherever I turned.

If you leave the crystal stream at the place where I had seen the born and the dead shimmering through the water's dream, and climb a little to a rise called Suntop, and stand beneath a particular oak, the silhouette of Cat Rock will be transformed. Here I gazed at the cliff and saw the distinct profile of the ancient, profound face of an Indian man staring north, the face of someone I would meet someday. He would not turn to me in my perplexity. I knew he would not answer me, but as I began to climb toward the warm and rounded cavern I knew was sculpted in the rock beneath his chin, I muttered once again, under my breath,

No, you will not leave me alone even after this.

Epilogue

The old man was speaking in the dark in his low, musical, sorrowful voice, just in front of the passageway to the deeper black of the dance lodge's interior. "I'm sorry," he said softly, "but I can't do it. I feel bad because I told you I would, I said come on over on Thursday night and we'll sing you that song and pray you that blessing by the center-post. I didn't know when I promised you that, that he would say I couldn't." He was standing in the dark with a young man who was struggling with a feeling of disappointment and desolation, looking at the ground. The old man placed his big hand on the other's shoulder. "But he's the boss. He's the one I have to listen too. And when I told him I was going to give you a blessing for telling the stories to people up there in Ono, he said 'Don't you do that! That guy already had a wife killed from messing around up in those Buttes, and if you go and pray for him and bless him with those songs and then something else happens to him, he'll blame you. Don't you do that!'"

"How did he know about all of that?" the younger man mumbled. "I never met him, I never saw him. Did someone tell him?"

"I dunno," said the old teacher. "That old guy knows all kinds of things. Anyway, I'm sorry I can't do for you what I said."

"Well," said the other, "it's all right. I'm on my own path up there in that mountain now, and I know very well that whatever I do there might have some effect I don't expect. I make offerings every time I go there, as you taught me, and I can offer my own prayer at the dance. I can put something by the center- post and pray."

"Yes, you can do that." The old man paused a bit, and said, "Anyway. I warned you already, I told you before, I don't see how you run around up there for so long, maybe stumbling across stuff you shouldn't a' stumbled across—you know those old doctors left all kinds of power things around up there—without something more happening to you". They stood for awhile in silence in the dark, listening to the wind in the oaks back on the old mound by the river and the yapping of the little dogs on the porches of the few small funky houses around the dance lodge.

The younger man continued, "And you know, a lot of things besides that—both light and dark—have happened to me up there. And however it may seem, the Mountain really does take care of me. But I didn't know much about all those powers then. Maybe if I had had an old grandfather like you to tell me about these things when I was a kid, it would have been different. Too late now. Damage is done!" He said this last humorously, smiling in the dark at his dubious joke.

"Well, I'm sorry anyway," the old man said, his voice sounding, as it always did, like an old song. "But you come Friday anyway, you come anyway with your wife and your kids, you come to the dance and sit in our family place." Then he was gone into the night toward the smudge of his porch light and his yapping dog. The other sat down on an uprighted oak-round that was waiting outside the dance lodge door by a pile of manzanita firewood for the upcoming three nights of dancing. Seventeen years had passed since that unspeakable violence on the Marysville street, and he had long *since learned that the Mountain was not really "dangerous" to him. Still he was startled and a little numbed at the reasons given for his mentor's refusal. While he was musing about this in the dark, he heard a door slam, footsteps on the gravel, and the form of the old man's daughter, recognized in silhouette, materialized near him. After only a few moments she began to speak in a melody of voice like that of her father's.*

"*Dad said he couldn't do it, didn't he,*" *she said.*

"*Yes. He said his old doctor up at Clearlake forbade it with some dire predictions.*"

She sniffed, and then made an unmistakable sound with her lips. "*That old man is Pomo,*" *she said with a note of authority.* "*He doesn't know anything about this mountain down here. And besides, as far as blessing-payers go, I dreamed this roundhouse here. Anyway, take this.*" *She pried open his fingers and tucked something into his palm.* "*This is medicine. Wormwood. It was gathered and sung over and blessed by a real Wintun woman doctor I know. She said to give it to you. She said if you're really supposed to be with this mountain and tell its stories it will help to keep you safe.*"

Watch for other books in the "Lord of the Valley" series:

The Heart of the People
Native wisdom, present dream, timeless power of a Sacred Mountain.

Geophany
Science, spirit and magic in the volcanic evolution of a landform.

The Mountain in our Midst
Sacred space in the market-place: personal discovery of the mountain's history and people.

Lord of the Valley
The mountain as Master: earth-form as the teacher of truth.

www.ingramcontent.com/pod-product-compliance
Lightning Source LLC
Chambersburg PA
CBHW051807040426
42446CB00007B/557